C'MON,
GET HAPPY...

C'MON, GET HAPPY...

DAVID CASSIDY

with CHIP DEFFAA

WARNER BOOKS

A Time Warner Company

Copyright © 1994 by DBC Enterprises, Inc.
All rights reserved.

Warner Books, Inc., 1271 Avenue of the Americas, New York, NY 10020

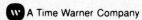 A Time Warner Company

Printed in the United States of America
First Printing: July 1994
10 9 8 7 6 5 4 3

Library of Congress Cataloging-in-Publication Data
Cassidy, David.
C'mon, get happy— : fear and loathing on the Partridge family bus / David Cassidy
with Chip Deffaa.
p.   cm.
ISBN 0-446-39531-5
1. Cassidy, David.   2. Singers—United States—Biography.   3. Actors—United
States—Biography.   I. Deffaa, Chip, 1951– .   II. Title.
ML420.C266A3   1994
782.42164'092—dc20
[B]   94-8573
                                                                        CIP
                                                                        MN

Cover design by Julia Kushnirsky
Cover photograph by Henry Diltz
Book design by Giorgetta Bell McRee

In the photo insert,
all color photographs by Henry Diltz;
all black and white photographs by Chip Deffaa.

With love for all who traveled the road with me . . .
and for those who got lost along the way.

Introduction

Somewhere between the sublime and ridiculous is a book called *C'mon Get Happy . . . Fear and Loathing on the Partridge Family Bus*. And as I, at the tender age of forty-three, have nearly completed this venture, I thought I might give you a little insight into my own take on it. I have always believed, and believe now, that any celebrity autobiography carries just slightly more significance, in terms of literary contribution, than does goose poop on the eastern shore of Maryland. So with that thought in mind, here goes.

All of us who claim we only want to share our experiences of strife and struggle since having donned this meaningful cloak of fame for any other reason than profit or the pursuit of more fame, are simply full of crap. All right, perhaps there is something of significance to be learned insofar as the human experience is concerned. I'll give us that. Perhaps what is unique about my own experience is that it (the fame) happened to me at a truly remarkable time on this planet, a time that we'll never see again. A time of innocence, of lost innocence, of helter skelter, of purple Osley, of Nixon, of Hendrix, of the Beatles, and yes, of *The Patridge Family*. A time of madness and psychedelia, of euphoria, and the silent moral majority. A time of indulgence, of overindulgence. As children of the sixties, we broke the dawn of the seventies with insatiable appetites for change. With reckless, careless abandon we boogied ourselves through the seventies. 'Cause that's the way uh-huh, uh-huh we liked it. No, we loved it. And now that it's long behind us, I can share some of those experiences with any of you out there who may be curious. I share these experiences with you from the perspective of no longer being that person I am writing about. Now ain't that mundo bizarro! My life has just gone through a tremendous metamorphosis. No apologies, no "Sorry folks, I did it, but I really didn't mean it," and it's nothing short of amazing that I remember so much of it so vividly. I guess it just really did have that much of an impact on me, too. With all this in mind, you're probably now thinking, "What is this book about then? Oh, I get it, it's a Hollywood kiss-and-tell book!" Hate to disappoint you, but if you're looking for sleaze, or you're looking for a list of celebrities I've slept with, you can put the book back on the shelf and consider it money you probably would have lost at the races anyway. My own unique celebrity experience in the 1970s, which I have been questioned endlessly about now for twenty years, has become something that I would like to put behind me at long last. Not that I am bitter about it, or remorseful about it, or hate it, or want nothing to do with it. Quite the contrary. I am amazed by it, amused by it, awed by it, and often proud of it. It's just that too big a piece of my "present" time is consumed discussing the past. I simply wish to live in the Now. Fortunately, for me, I have a "big time" Now. Now is where my happiness lives. But shit, did it take me a long time to get over that hump.

From time to time people have asked me, "Don't you get sick of being asked the same questions over and over again about what happened when you were on *The Partridge Family* and being a teen idol?" I've tried answering them this way: It would be like every person who met you, who was introduced to you, who had a reference to you from the four years you spent in college, and the only thing they wanted to ask you about was that great touchdown you made in the closing seconds of that game one Saturday in October half your life ago. Of course it was great, of course you'd never forget it, of course at that moment it seemed like the world was focused on you and you alone. It was your moment. But for you it's over, and you don't play football anymore. You aren't in college anymore. And as much as they'd like to see you in the cleats, pads, and helmet again, it just ain't gonna happen twenty years later. And you, having fond memories of the experience, have decided to tell anyone who should ever ask the "What was it like?" question to "Turn to page 257 in your handbook. I think you'll find the answer there." So, you see, this is my way of completion. I ain't gonna work on Maggie's farm no more. There has been catharsis in this, and yes, even nostalgia for me, too. I just thought I might tell you before you read through me, I really do love you all for being there with me, and for still being here with me now. Happy trails.

C'MON,
GET HAPPY...

CHAPTER 1

You want to know my most vivid childhood memory?

It's early 1956. I think I'm five, nearly six, and I'm playing with a couple of my friends out in the street in front of our house at 23 Elm Street in West Orange, New Jersey. They begin to taunt me with that casual cruelness kids can have: "Hey, Wartie, your parents are divorced." They called me Wartie because my grandfather's last name was Ward. And at this time in my life, that's with whom I was living. And with my mom as well. But they just hadn't gotten around to telling me about the divorce.

"No, they aren't," I respond, unnerved. I had never heard the word "divorce" before, but somehow I knew what it meant. "Maybe in a play they are, but not in real life." My parents, Jack Cassidy and Evelyn Ward, were actors—not very successful ones—but they'd done plays and musicals, sometimes together, mostly apart.

"They're divorced," one of my friends assures me, like it's a well-known fact. But nobody I know has parents who are divorced. That just doesn't exist in my world. A world that suddenly has an uneasiness. I think that was the first time I can remember feeling naked. I remember running into the house for assurance.

Even though I'm sure my mom will say, "Don't be silly," I ask her hesitantly if she and my dad are divorced. She takes a long breath and says, "Why don't you ask your father that? You're going to see him next weekend." I say okay. That was enough for me to feel whole again, at least until I saw my dad.

I don't see a lot of my father lately. He's usually "on the road," doing plays, as my mother often explains to me. The plays keep him very busy—so busy, in fact, that even when he promises he's going to come visit me, he isn't always able to keep his promise. I'm used to that. After all, this is Jack Cassidy we're talking about, folks.

My mom and I live with my grandparents at their house, where they've lived since 1918. My grandfather is more of a father to me than my own dad. Born in 1889, he's worked for public service all his adult life, reading meters. My grandmother Ethel never missed a Sunday at Holy Trinity Church. (Neither did I; they had me singing in the choir as soon as I was old enough.) She and my aunt Marion and other relatives have had factory jobs.

Our neighborhood is purely middle class, very much white Anglo-Saxon Protestant. Very church-oriented. Elm Street has unpretentious, closely spaced single-family homes, with the clotheslines in the back. There are people across the street from us who keep chickens in their backyard. The "rag man" comes down the street collecting people's old rags and bottles. My friends' parents are carpenters, plumbers, policemen. I'm the youngest kid on the block and the only one who has begun school at Eagle Rock. They have all been going to Our Lady of Lourdes, the Catholic elementary school across the street. It's a small solid kind of a place. My mom never worried about me walking to Eagle Rock Elementary School or running off to play at Eagle Rock Reservation. Although, as I think back on those years now, it's almost as if that was another person's life. For Hollywood (gasp) distorted who I am.

I remember waiting for my father to visit that weekend so I could ask him the important question. And him driving up in grand style in a shiny new Cadillac. So Jack. Even if he didn't have much money, he looked the part. If he had fifty dollars, my mother used to say he'd spend forty on a suit for himself and leave ten for us to live on. When he arrived, I remember him bundling me into a bulky overcoat—it was winter—and saying exuberantly, with a wave of his hand, "We're going to New York!" He could make it sound as if he had just invented New York, and was about to make a present of it to you. He had so much charm, you couldn't help but love him.

We lived less than twenty miles from New York City. We drove there—we were on Route 3, passing the marshlands of Secaucus, before I finally asked him the big question. I knew he would say no and then everything would be exactly the way it was before my friends started taunting me. But instead he paused, drew his breath, and said yes.

Whatever problems I have today in trusting people; whatever problems I have in dealing with rejection, with loss—and I'm hypersensitive about abandonment, about needing people around me to be consistent and loving—have their origins in that moment.

When he said that he and my mom were divorced, I could hardly pull myself together. It felt like every part of my body came unglued at that one moment and began to shake and convulse out of pain, fear, and rejection.

I was stunned that he had decided to leave me and my mother—and hadn't even bothered telling me. I've never completely recovered from that. I still walk around feeling abandoned and deceived. They had been divorced for over two years.

It couldn't have taken much time to drive the rest of the way into Manhattan, but in my memory it took four hours.

He said he would still come to see me. But throughout my growing-up years, he never did come around very much to see me again. I felt shunned—like I did something wrong. I was a very sensitive kid. My father made some serious, dark imprints on me that I still to this day stumble over.

My father got married again in August of 1956, to actress Shirley Jones, whose career was going much better than his. She had starring roles in the films of *Oklahoma!* (1955) and *Carousel* (1956). She and my father had met in a stage production of *Oklahoma!* They made their home in New York until 1957, then moved to California, which meant I saw even less of my dad. And he began getting some guest shots on television.

My dad and Shirley lived quite comfortably, even rich, thanks largely to Shirley's earnings. She went on to appear in movies like *April Love* (1957), *Never Steal Anything Small* (1959), *Elmer Gantry*, for which she won an Academy Award as Best Supporting Actress (1960), *Two Rode Together* (1961), and *The Music Man* (1962). After she won her Academy Award, they moved into a forty-room mansion, on five acres in Bel Air, that had belonged to Merle Oberon; it must be worth $20 million today. I remember visiting my father once in the early sixties and counting the shoes in his closet: he had 104 pairs! Even at the peak of my success, I don't think I ever had more than five pairs. I'm happy with two. But he was so self-indulgent. A self-absorbed man, I came to understand as I got older, who expected everyone in his life—his children, his wife, the people he worked with—to deal with him on his terms. His reality. The world according to Jack.

Yet, for all his flaws, I worshipped him. He could be an incredibly affectionate man. And I've never known anyone with as much charisma. Being around him was an intense experience—in both the good times and the bad. As a child, I always wanted to be like him. I had known since I was three and a half, when I saw him in the Broadway show *Wish You Were Here*—standing on the stage, with his arms spread out, singing, and everybody clapping for him—that I wanted to be a performer, just like him. And as I grew older, maybe a part of me even believed that if I became a performer like he was, it would bring us the closeness we never had.

As a child, I always loved going into New York to see him appear in Broadway shows. I have wonderful impressions of show business inextricably linked in my memory with him—as bright and gay and buoyant. My primary childhood memories of West Orange—colored by my dad's absence so much of the time—are that it was gray and drab. As a boy as young as six or seven, I secretly felt that I belonged much more in that bright-lights world of my father's in New York than in West Orange. My mother felt that way, too. That's why she left home and headed to Broadway.

A lot of people I've met over the years seem to assume that Shirley Jones and Jack Cassidy raised me. This is far from the truth. When Shirley and I appeared in *The Partridge Family*, the network got a lot of publicity mileage out of the fact that Shirley played my mother on the show and was my stepmother in real life. Even today, I'll meet fans who assume that I had this fabulous showbiz upbringing, growing up in the home with movie stars Shirley Jones and Jack Cassidy. They don't picture me back in West Orange. My father balked at paying child support, claiming he couldn't afford it. My mom had to take him to court a couple of times; he had washed his hands of us. (But when he and my mom had first gotten married, he had thought nothing of sponging off my mom's parents, living with them rent-free.)

I was sort of scrawny and looked young for my age. I had to

wear corrective lenses for a while, due to a wandering eye caused by two deformed eye muscles. Eventually, when I was eleven, I had an operation to fix it. But I never developed great reading skills. I wasn't a good student. I clowned around a lot in school. I found ways to make myself the center of attention. Like being a fuckup.

I always felt somehow "different" from my classmates. Beginning in West Orange. It wasn't just that I was the only kid in school whose parents were in *show business* (that was weird enough to my friends), or the only kid I knew whose parents were divorced (which carried a stigma in the fifties); I just remember feeling "different" in some way I can't fully explain.

Shirley Jones remembers: "David had a lot of difficulty as a child. He was a very sensitive little boy. He was not very open to me because he felt I'd really taken his father away. So my meetings with him were a week or two in the summer and maybe a few days over the Christmas holidays when he would come and stay with us. He was always very polite, very sweet—almost to a fault—because he was trying to be on his best behavior. His father was a big disciplinarian. Jack was really from the old school of spare the rod and spoil the child."

I think when my father periodically decided to play disciplinarian in my life, he was trying to make up for the fact that he was so rarely in my life at all.

What other early memories of my father do I have? Well, I can remember him taking me to a restaurant and downing seventeen Scotch and sodas. He seemed to handle it, back in those days; he just seemed to be in very good cheer. His mood would become even more expansive. You felt good being around him. As I got older, though, I realized he was an alcoholic (even if he never acknowledged it)—as was one of his brothers, as was their father, William Cassidy.

My father wasn't the type to say to me, "I'm proud of you," or to give me much confidence. He wasn't good with stuff like that.

But I really adored him. So, I might add, did my younger brothers, Shaun, Patrick, and Ryan—the three sons he had by Shirley— although we would all suffer various scars that are the consequences, over the years, of his habitually putting his own desires first. My dad had such a vivid presence, such great flair. I don't think my mom ever got over him. And even though my dad's marriage to Shirley Jones also eventually ended in divorce (in 1975), I don't think Shirley ever really got over him, either. Or my brothers. Or me.

The reason I now spend time every day with my own son is that I was cheated out of that time with my father. Everything he did with me I now do the opposite with Beau. I couldn't live with myself any other way.

I've spent at least five years of my life—three and a half of them intensely, three times a week—in psychoanalysis, trying to heal myself, to rid myself of some of the darkness and pain I've felt through the years as a result of my father's selfishness. Oh, God, this is beginning to sound so damn depressing. Honestly, it ain't all like this, folks.

CHAPTER 2

In 1961, four years after my father moved out to California, my mom and I followed.

My mom did it partly because she figured it would be good for her acting career. She had had some success in New York—the high point being when she succeeded Gwen Verdon in George Abbott's production of *New Girl in Town* on Broadway—and it was reasonable for her to want to try Hollywood. That's where the money was. The big show.

But mostly, she moved for my sake. She knew I needed more contact with my father. My grandfather, for all his virtues, couldn't really take the place of my dad. I was growing up wild and undisciplined. My mom was great, but she was a lax disciplinarian. If she was tied up with a play in New York or on the road, she couldn't always be there for me. I was getting into a fair amount of mischief.

A psychologist might say I was "acting out" my anger at my dad's having abandoned us. My mom was worried I might be on the road to becoming a juvenile delinquent. Baby, she was right.

So we made the move west in '61, when I was eleven. (For the record, I was born April 12, 1950.) I'd spent summers and Christmases with my dad since 1958, so California wasn't really new to me. I loved the idea of living there.

We moved to a little street called Crestview Court in West Los Angeles, right off Beverly Glen. It was a small Spanish-style house—maybe twelve hundred square feet. I began elementary school in the fifth grade at Fairburn in West Los Angeles.

My mom was getting some acting jobs—in plays and occasional TV shows like *Ben Casey* or *Dr. Kildare*—to pay the rent. Barely. Then in 1962 she married director Elliot Silverstein. She'd been seeing him for about five years in New York. He was then working primarily in television, but would shortly make his mark directing such feature films as *Cat Ballou* (1965), *The Happening* (1967), and *A Man Called Horse* (1970). My mom pretty much gave up her acting career after she married him, and tried to spend more time being my mother and his wife. I liked him well enough—but when you already have a father, there's your father and there's everybody else. Elliot tried very hard to fill the void the first couple of years. I know it must not have been easy for him.

It's hard even now to compare my father with other dads. I know he wasn't great in a lot of ways: he was terrible. He wasn't there for any of my Little League games. He promised, but never showed up. I can still hear his voice, telling me over the phone, "Honey, I'm not going to be able to come to this one—but remember, I'll be there in spirit." (He only actually made it to one of my games, for half an hour.) Gradually Shirley and I became a little closer—I came to see that she was really a warm, giving, and consistent person—because she recognized that my father was so unreliable and she didn't want me to get hurt. She knew who he was: he was the same with her kids, Shaun, Pat, and Ryan.

Around Christmastime in 1962, when I was twelve, my father went on an overnight father-son camping trip with me. Because he'd disappointed me so many times before, my mom and Shirley rammed him till he had to make the decision to go with me. It was a camping trip in the snow, up in the San Bernardino Mountains at a Boy Scout camp. Now, my dad is used to staying at digs like the Plaza and the Sherry-Netherland hotels when he's in New York. He lives in a huge mansion with a pool, guesthouse, servants' quarters—the works—in Bel Air, California.

My dad shows up for the camping trip dressed like fucking David Niven. He's going camping with me, wearing a brand-new outfit—sheepskin gloves, boots, silk scarf, brand-new—he must have bought them at the most expensive store in Beverly Hills. His hair, as always, is absolutely perfect. Everybody else's dad is just, ya know, dad. Flannel shirt and jeans. But not Jack. We drive up to the mountains, to the forest, and we start to build our tents, get our sleeping bags, sit around the campfire, and have the scoutmaster tell stories. About nine o'clock we say good night. It's freezing by now. All the fathers go into the cabin together. Good night! I'm thinking, *My dad in that funky cabin?* I don't know.

At about 6 A.M. we all get up. The other dads start coming out of the cabin. The first thing they do is look at me, smile, pat me on the back, and say, "Your dad. What a guy. He kept us up all night, telling us jokes and stories. What a father! It must be great growing up with him. I've never met anyone like him!"

And I'm thinking, *Yeah, it's really great. I've seen him like four times. You're talking about my dad?* The other dads come out, laughing, saying, "Your father's in there holding court. Oh, by the way, don't get concerned when you see his hand. Apparently he picked up a hot poker in the middle of the night. He was building a fire for us." Pure romance, my dad.

Apparently he'd brought some booze with him. He was passing the Scotch around while the kids slept. My dad sat around the fire telling show business stories. Just being one of the guys.

I mean, sit around and tell showbiz stories—he could do that for days! He had such a cunning wit. He knew seemingly everybody in the business, from Cole Porter to Stephen Sondheim. I was proud of him, but our one big weekend wound up becoming his big weekend. I don't remember the "us" part. He had a need I couldn't quite understand, to always be the center of attention—an insatiable need to be "on."

My father began taking me with him on summer-stock tours, for maybe a week at a time, when he could—which sure beat hanging around Los Angeles over summer vacation. I not only got to see more of my dad, I saw different parts of America, and different parts of show business. I became a savvy, sophisticated kid.

Looking back, I'm sure it bothered my dad that his career was then so greatly overshadowed by Shirley's, although he wouldn't have admitted that. She was in demand for films; he wasn't. In Hollywood he was still, in effect, "Mr. Shirley Jones." (That would begin to change when he starred in the Broadway musical *She Loves Me* in 1963–64 and won a Tony Award; after that, his career would take off.) In 1962, in contrast to Shirley, Jack Cassidy was not considered a star. But he expressed great pride to me in being what he termed a "working actor." It was an honorable profession, he stressed. Just not an easy one.

He was doing enough guest roles on TV shows by then that people were just beginning to know his face. In 1961 and '62 alone he appeared in episodes of *Alfred Hitchcock Presents*, *Wagon Train*, *Hawaiian Eye*, *Bronco*, *Hennesey*, *Maverick*, *The Real McCoys*, *Cheyenne*, *Surfside 6*, and *77 Sunset Strip*, and also lent his distinctive, cultured voice to the sound track of a cartoon special, *Mr. Magoo's Christmas*. That's a lot of work.

He was recognized in the business as a highly competent, versatile actor. It had taken him many years of practicing his craft, he explained to me, to reach that point. And if I chose to make acting my career (as I said I intended to), I could expect a similarly long, slow struggle to master my craft and gain respect and recognition from my peers. I accepted that reality.

In his early years, when he was in the chorus of many shows, my father acknowledged to me, his acting had been considered quite wooden. He had initially gotten by on his splendid Irish tenor voice (although he abused it by drinking and smoking too much) and his appearance. His features were near perfect—leaning more toward pretty, perhaps, than handsome. (One critic aptly described him as "almost too good looking.")

Years of very hard work at his craft—for he had appeared in his first Broadway show when he was just fifteen—had paid off for him. He had gradually gotten much better. I heeded his words. When I imagined my own future, I was certain it would be just like my father's: a slow but steady development as a not necessarily famous—but respected—"working actor."

My dad didn't have to tell me that he had become a creditable actor: I saw proof every time I was with him. He was always acting—and quite grandly. The Jack Cassidy persona the world saw was probably his finest acting job of all. He created that character—dashing, debonair, devil-may-care. If you remember seeing my father from any of his talk-show appearances with Johnny Carson, Mike Douglas, or Merv Griffin, I'm sure you remember this ultra-suave, charming, refined man. He actually grew up in a tough section of Jamaica, Queens, New York. By fifteen he'd quit school, and—lying about his age—worked as an elevator operator, limousine driver, and anything else necessary to get by, in between acting jobs. He used his charm (and whatever else it took) to cultivate relationships that would help him advance in his career. I think he cultivated the voice by watching movies as a teen. He worshipped Barrymore's style and profile, I think. He was his prototype for creating the Jack Cassidy we all saw.

He came from working-class, Irish Catholic stock. According to family lore, his mother, Lotte, was a really hard nut. Everyone said she had ice water running through her veins. She bore my father exceptionally late in life, when she was forty-eight (in 1928). She was unhappy to have this unwanted change-of-life child; she seemed embarrassed by him, as if she believed a woman her age wasn't supposed to be having sex anymore, much less children. And she rejected him, handing him over to a woman a few houses away, who nursed him on her tit and looked after him. My father, I'm sure, was damaged goods from the moment his mother rejected him. The various psychological problems he had, including that insatiable need of his for attention, no doubt had their origins right there. As did the full-fledged mental illness he would develop later in life. He once told me he could never remember his mother ever kissing him.

His father, Willie Cassidy, a railroad engineer, was by all accounts a wonderful man. I remember as a lad of about eight or nine that he always made me laugh when I would visit. A big drinker—that ran in the family—but lovable. He had a remarkable sense of humor. And he was a notorious rogue. Eventually I began to hear talk from various people that my own father also did his share of philandering. Nothing people told me about my father has ever really surprised me. He was a larger-than-life kind of guy.

We clashed a lot maybe because our personalities were so alike. But it was always exciting being around him. He heightened every experience, positive or negative.

As I spent more time with him, I came to realize there was

one person whose opinions he valued—whose esteem he sought—even more than Shirley's. And that was Ruth Aarons. He worshipped her. And she him.

Ruth was his and Shirley's manager. It's as if she was almost always a part of our family. And she always took an interest in me. I found her entertaining, engaging, and funny. (As I grew older, I realized she was also lonely—and could be quite manipulative.) She looked kind of tomboyish and was almost always by herself. But attractive. People presumed she was gay; only at the very end of her life was I aware there was a man in her life. She could talk to me easily, about things that really interested me—music, sports, and so on—in a way that other adults couldn't.

And there didn't seem to be anything about show business she didn't know—which shouldn't have been surprising, since both her father, Alex Aarons, and her grandfather Alfred Aarons had been famed theatrical producers. Her father, in partnership with Vinton Freedley, had produced such smash Broadway hits as *Lady, Be Good!*, *Oh, Kay!*, *Funny Face, Hold Everything*, and *Girl Crazy* and had built and owned New York's Alvin Theater. As a little girl, she had sat under the piano at parties at which the likes of George Gershwin and Cole Porter entertained. Though her father lost his fortune in the stock market crash of 1929, while she was in her teens, she had become a table-tennis world champion. By the late 1940s she had become a theatrical manager. I believe she may have been the first. She had very few clients, but didn't need many. They were all successful. She was so personally involved in the development and maintenance of her clients' careers, most stayed with her forever. They knew her touch was golden. And she would do anything for them. By the early 1960s, she was working with Celeste Holm, George Chakiris, Shirley Jones, Janis Paige, and my father.

She was the only one of my father's friends I could really talk with. She was vibrant, wise, and sophisticated. Class, real class. Someday she would be my manager, and consequently one of the most important people in my life. But in the early 1960s that was still a half dozen years or so in the future. She was still just Auntie Ruth.

CHAPTER
3

Maybe I should have been in school that day, but I used to cut classes pretty often. Bored mostly. I was walking through Westwood Village, in Los Angeles, when I heard the news that President Kennedy had been shot. I was thirteen years old on that day, November 22, 1963. That day still carries a certain weight for me. It's the sense of loss again. I couldn't believe we didn't have our President anymore.

As people heard the news, the streets emptied. People who'd been out shopping quietly went home. I'd never seen Westwood totally deserted like that.

That date marks the beginning of what we think of as "the sixties"—those turbulent years when everything in our society seemed to be changing. Up until then, it had been damned near inconceivable that anyone would kill a President. And then Martin

Luther King, Bobby Kennedy, and Malcolm X were all killed. Did the shooting of JFK make it easier for others to think of—and carry out—assassinations? Did it somehow make it easier for many of us—in ways large or small—to consider breaking laws or codes of conduct? Did it contribute to the unraveling of the social fabric that went on throughout the sixties? Back in the fifties it was as if nobody—except real criminals—broke a law. We all stayed in line. Butch haircuts, pressed shirts. And now, in the sixties, all laws, all rules, all codes of conduct, seemed suddenly open to question. Restraints were loosening throughout society.

A lot of the changes in those years were excessive. There was an element of madness loose in our culture—think of the killings, the lives lost to drug overdoses. Tune in, turn on, drop out. But, to me, the sixties were about freedom. There was the Free Speech Movement. And of course the struggle for civil rights for blacks. The sixties also saw the birth of the modern feminist movement and the gay rights movement. Everyone was seeking freedom and justice. Drugs were perceived as something that would help liberate us, expand our consciousness.

Did I feel a part of that growing movement, that counterculture? You bet. Was I antiwar? You better believe it! Nobody understood what the fuck America was doing in Vietnam. My mother and I were both strongly opposed to the war; she said if I were to be drafted, we'd move to Canada. I couldn't imagine myself going to Vietnam; I wasn't exactly the military type. Fortunately, when the time came, I lucked out in the first draft lottery, when I was nineteen, so I was never called to serve. The peace symbol really meant something to me—to all my friends. I was at the time totally "unpatriotic." To me, a child of the sixties, a "patriot" was somebody who blindly supported the government's increasingly militaristic policies.

The Establishment was trying to keep the younger generation

in line, to keep the lid on all of the growing pressures for change. Adults seemed threatened by longhaired youths. Back then, wearing your hair long—and I was one of the first in my school to start doing so—symbolized some degree of allegiance to the counterculture. It spoke of who you were. Adults wanted to control how kids wore their hair. It was as if, by doing that, they could control the kids' thinking. If every hair was cut short and matted down with Brylcreem, then rebellious impulses could be similarly controlled. My stepfather, a graduate of Yale, naturally didn't approve of my letting my hair grow longer. (He got even more upset when I later dyed it blond—the gap between us grew wider and wider as the sixties wore on.)

When I entered University High School in 1965, I was ordered to the vice-principal's office because the length of my hair was questionable. He made me shake my head in front of him, saying that if a single hair on my head moved, I wouldn't be allowed to enroll. And it wasn't even that long then. But that's how seriously they were cracking down. They were drawing a line.

I was already someone who was anti-establishment. So was my good friend Kevin Hunter—we'd hang out in Westwood Village every day after school—and some other guys, Ross Nogen, David Greene. We were wild. We were the rebels. We didn't like that we had to dress the way they dictated if we wanted to get an education. So when we first heard about "love-ins"—celebrations for hippies and for people who aligned themselves with that philosophy, where any behavior or form of dress (or undress) was acceptable—you can bet they sounded more attractive to us than school.

Clothes were a big issue. My generation started wearing bell bottoms because everyone in the older generation wore straight pants. Adults today may laugh at bell bottoms, but when we first wore them, they meant something to us. It was all about freedom, about self-expression.

As far as I was concerned, California was *the* place to be in the 1960s. It was really the hub in terms of the whole social/sexual revolution. What people in the Midwest were reading about in magazines, or following via radio and TV, we were witnessing and experiencing. My appetite to be a part of the culture of the sixties, the new social culture, the new musical culture, was really keen.

My musical heroes, through the sixties, included the Beatles, the Beach Boys, Eric Clapton, John Mayall and the Bluesbreakers, B.B. King, Albert King, Albert Collins, Marvin Gaye, Otis Redding. And of course Jimi Hendrix. He was the greatest performer of the era. I saw him four or five times. He was a sexual magnet.

Steve Ross, a friend who played guitar in the first garage band I was in (and would be an important friend for many years to come), turned me on to guitar. We could jam on a basic blues or a Hendrix number for an hour and a half at a time. I'm sure it stunk, but to us it was the stuff.

When I was in bands, we started playing Beatles songs, then went to blues songs, then to Jimi Hendrix songs. Personally I progressed from being a real pop music fan like an average kid to a rhythm and blues music fan—I was looking for something deeper, more authentic—to a hard-core acid-rock, Hendrix, Clapton, Jeff Beck, Peter Green, John Mayall, Paul Butterfield, Mike Bloomfield type of fan. Music reflected all the social change that went on in the sixties, the whole social revolution.

It's ironic that, because of *The Partridge Family*, I became publicly identified with a kind of sweet, lightweight, mainstream pop music. I really didn't listen to music like that *at all*. I became the antithesis of mainstream pop. I followed the blues and the acid-rock bands—the very first FM artists. Being on the cutting edge of pop culture was definitely what I wanted. I mean, when you go to see Hendrix five times—and everybody there's high, all 18,000 people—Hendrix was about as far from mainstream pop as you could get. Some teens in the sixties may have been buying slick little commercial pop records like "Yummy, Yummy, Yummy, I've Got Love in my Tummy" and "Chewy, Chewy," but not us. In the sixties my friends and I went to rock concerts and saw Cream, with people selling—and some even giving away—acid. I went to a party up in Laurel Canyon one night and Janis Joplin was there. She was a big deal at that time . . . maybe late '66 to '67. But she was there getting high like everybody else. Sunset Strip in Hollywood was a gathering place for people who shared that philosophy and were really committed to changing. Hendrix and Joplin were role models for teenagers in the revolution that I identified with.

Drugs, of course, became a big part of the youth movement. We came to think of drugs as recreational, fun, something that could expand your mind, make you more loving, and enhance sex. And drugs were new—something my generation did that, generally speaking, the previous generations didn't do.

When I was fifteen, a friend of mine who was a few years older offered me and one of my really good friends from school, Sam Hyman, our first joints. I already knew how to smoke, of course— I'd been smoking regular cigarettes since I was thirteen and would continue to do so until I was twenty—but this was something different. Pot was just coming onto the scene, as far as kids my age were concerned. None of my friends had yet seen pot or even talked about it. Don't forget, this was 1965—we're talking about a period just slightly pre-psychedelia, pre–Haight-Ashbury, pre–*Life* magazine's reporting that people were experimenting with LSD, which was how I first learned that LSD existed, as a curious ninth grader. Drugs would really explode onto the scene in 1966 and '67. In 1965 I didn't know much about marijuana at all, except I knew that there were some jazz musicians like Gene Krupa who'd messed with it; I'd seen Sal Mineo (who was actually a friend—I'll get to that later) in *The Gene Krupa Story*.

The first time I smoked a joint, I felt like a real derelict. Sam and I had gone to visit this unbalanced guy, down by the railroad tracks around Sepulveda, where a lot of Mexicans lived. The guy had an alcoholic mother; Sam and I brought her a bottle of Cutty Sark as our friend had suggested, so she wouldn't care what any of us were doing. We went around to the back of the house and he showed us these two wilted, hand-rolled cigarettes. I thought they looked bizarre, really sleazy. But I was a curious, adventurous lad. I rarely had anything to do except go to school. And this older guy showed us how to smoke pot—inhaling real deeply, you know, and holding it in. And I was profoundly affected by it. I got hammered. Over the next few years, I was to discover I was deeply sensitive to almost any kind of drug.

Eventually I told my mom I smoked dope. She surprised me when she told me that she and my dad had actually tried it, back in their early theater days—they had gotten some from a musician friend—and so she knew it wasn't hell, although she hadn't cared for it. I was impressed that my mom thought so "young." Because she'd been brought up in the theater, I guess, nothing really shocked her. She was open-minded compared to most adults. So she was really my friend, I felt then. My pals from school all used to tell me how cool my mom was. She was really good-looking, too, which was probably impressive. She looked like Elizabeth Taylor. She was a knockout.

In those days there was usually a huge difference between teens and adults, who'd all grown up before the advent of rock and roll. In the sixties, when the whole social/sexual revolution was going on, there were light-years between people who were merely ten years apart in age. Most adults were from a whole different mind-set than the kids. That's where "Never trust anyone over thirty" came from. Nowadays, there often isn't much of a gap between someone forty-five and thirty, or between someone thirty and twenty. But in those days ten years were usually huge.

As a teenager in high school, I found myself experimenting

with all sorts of drugs as opportunities arose; that became an important part of my life, like part of my zest for living. I was reckless, wild. We were young kids experimenting with pot, hash, psychedelics, mescaline, THC, speed, Tuinal, and more. In 1966–67 I'd take speed maybe once a month, or once every couple of weeks, and sometimes go on a binge for two or three days. Maybe some diet pills or something. My body always reacted violently to amphetamines, though; I was never able to handle them well. Everybody I knew in school experimented with drugs at the ages of sixteen and seventeen, in 1966 and '67.

In 1967 I hitchhiked up to Haight-Ashbury with my friend Kevin Hunter. We spent a couple of days and nights there smoking weed and taking acid. We hitched up there only because we'd seen it on the news. We'd heard it was the place to be and we considered ourselves to be tuned-in guys. I had just finished eleventh grade in high school. I guess I looked about twelve. But I had pretty long hair and I felt a part of the whole hippie movement, the whole social/sexual revolution thing. Kevin and I figured we were just like those older guys who were into the "turn on, tune in, drop out" concept, except that we were, you know, still living at home. We were both about to start twelfth grade at the Rexford School in a couple of weeks.

We stayed at this place right off the Haight. The door was open. Hippies everywhere. It was a crash pad—a small room with people sleeping on the floor. A huge bowl in the middle of the room had methedrine in it. People were fixing methedrine, cooking it, and passing the syringe around in the middle of this room of filthy people.

There was one really weird-looking guy, wearing a white robe. He was ninety-eight pounds; he looked like a skeleton. He was clutching this bottle that must have held a hundred pills, like a miser with a purse. Every so often, he'd flip the top open, take a couple of these pills, then flip it back closed. His mind was obviously lost already.

We crashed in this room on the floor that night. In the morning the guy was gone. But his shoes were there along with the bottle that had maybe two little pills left in it. I wondered what had happened to him from taking so many pills; I wondered if he had died. Nobody knew.

But that day in S.F. we were at Golden Gate Park, where as we walked in someone handed us some purple Osley acid. Free. We were in the summer of love at a love-in, and I think either the Jefferson Airplane or Iron Butterfly was playing. We were too ripped to know.

We hitched back home. Kevin and I had hardly slept the whole weekend, maybe two or three hours a night, and we were blown away from the acid and the hitching. I went up to my room and slept for twenty-one hours.

LSD wasn't even illegal when I first heard about it. Trying it was about living that culture, the cutting edge of the sixties. I experimented with LSD and peyote buttons. I can remember holding a friend of mine's hand during a bad trip. I watched people who were not terribly secure really lose it.

I knew a lot of people who took acid every day. I took acid perhaps ten times, maybe a little more. I even drove once while on LSD. I don't ever want to do that again. That was actually the very first time I took LSD, in Palm Springs over Easter vacation, 1966. I was driving my mom's 1959 Olds convertible and got stopped by a cop for having a busted taillight. The cop started searching the car and I went into this "golly, shucks, gee, Officer, I'm not feeling well—can't we hurry this up" kind of routine. I managed to seep a little sympathetic sunshine from the guy—I mean, he actually bought that I was just a really nice kid with a busted taillight— and he let me go with just a simple ticket. He couldn't tell I had taken LSD. It hadn't really kicked in much yet. But by the time I went to get something to eat, I was hallucinating vividly; the hamburger was dancing on my plate while the french fries were standing up and conducting music, which made me laugh so hard I couldn't eat them. Then I went back to my hotel room—and found cops were busting in. I had been staying with some LSD dealers, among others—a lot of kids, crowded into a room over spring break—and they'd attracted attention to themselves.

I got a girl to drive me away from there, fast. Before we got too far, though, we happened upon the scene of an accident—this red '65 GTO with a totally smashed-in front end, and the driver, covered with blood, his head horribly damaged, screaming in pain. I'd never seen a sight so gruesome in my life, and by then I was really peaking on the LSD, which increased my agitation. The girl driving the car I was in started screaming, too; the guy was obviously going to die. Since then, I've always had an intensified fear of auto accidents, a fear I'd never had before.

I think my psychedelic experiences, by and large, were with the wrong people or in the wrong environments. If you're not in good shape to begin with, believe me, LSD's not going to make it any better for you. Some people have told me that they enjoyed blissful, beautiful, magical psychedelic trips. But I didn't. I think I took it often with guys who were lost—the most insecure, sad, lonely, desperate guys I could have picked—just kids from school or people I'd met hanging around a pool hall I used to go to. One druggy friend I knew had tried to commit suicide a few times.

I had an appetite for living on the edge back then. It was a big deal to steal things and put them back in different places. When I was thirteen, I'd take a bike on my way home from school, maybe paint it or fix it up a little, use it for a month or so, and then guilt would take over and I'd return it. Awhile later, I'd swipe another one and do the same. I'd always return them, though. I just couldn't live with myself.

Stealing wasn't really a big part of my life, though. It was more like, if I saw a rule of any sort, I'd think, *Let's see, how can I break this? Or bend this?* Being told not to do something was an enticement for me.

My mom had me go to a psychologist for a period of time when I was using drugs. In the sixties that was considered a very sophisticated, intellectual way of dealing with children. I basically told the psychologist what I wanted to, so that my mother would wind up getting told I needed more love, trust, and understanding. It was completely manipulation on my part, not analysis. As far as I was concerned, the only problems I had were, how was I going to get through the school year without doing any homework and how could I pull the wool over my parents' eyes so I could continue having the lifestyle I wanted? Because there was no way I could ever, like, be serious about biology.

I was really very good at being a teenager. I was good at getting away with shit—staying out all night messing around, lying to my parents, and trying desperately to act older than I was—until the arrival of Judgment Day, the day report cards came. I wound up having to go to summer school between tenth and eleventh grades, and then again between eleventh and twelfth grades, and then still again right after twelfth. I got kicked out of two high schools for cutting classes. My parents didn't know what to do with me.

I wound up getting sent to what they called continuation school, which is what they had in Los Angeles for incorrigibles who were too young to legally drop out of school. There were students with a lot of emotional problems. There were a lot of losers. I saw guys who brought guns and knives to school, guys whose future was clearly San Quentin.

I couldn't take the continuation school any longer, so I begged my mom, "There's a private school called Rexford that Kevin is going to now, where they let you grow your hair, where they let you be who you are. They encourage individuality. Let me try it there and I promise I will work hard." I went to Rexford for my last year and a half and I actually flourished a little bit. There were only five to twelve kids in a class. I began drama classes, too, which I loved. They had no "frills" like that in continuation school. The teachers related to me. It sparked my interest.

Kevin was already going there when I enrolled midway through my junior year. He was wild—but he also had a lot of gifts. He had a great mind, was an artist and a very good writer. He'd make up all these great characters with great names—like Jackson Snipe. I mean, who could forget a name like *Jackson Snipe?* Kevin had a tape recorder. We'd get high and write and act these tapes and radio shows together. A lot of our creativity, we believed, came out of beer and drugs. We played two homosexuals in some really silly one-act plays. We wrote plays together, which we performed in drama class and for our graduation. Kevin was just a great, great pal, and really a talent. He was different; special. We did so much fucking around together. We were headed—or so we presumed—in pretty much the same direction.

Kevin and I knew a couple of heroin addicts. By our senior year in high school, 1967–68, Kevin was occasionally getting high on heroin himself. And I of course tried it with him. Once. I was into experiencing as much as I could back then. And if your friends do, you do. So we went out and bought a dime bag of heroin and shared it. I never used a needle. I just snorted it. I was very heavy. Very dark and slow. I could see how you become a human wasteland very quickly, and I wanted no part of it. Way too bleak.

Kevin and I also liked doing poppers—I'm talking about amyl nitrite, the fumes of which produce an intense, short-lived rush. I remember one time when we were in a school play. Right before we were supposed to go on, performing for all our parents and teachers and everybody, we popped an amy. We walked out onstage in our costumes for the play—and blew it completely. I mean, we were in hysterics, just bent over, knocking things over, bumping into people. It was more like a slapstick routine. Embarrassing now looking back. The adults may not have been too impressed, but we were having a good time, and that was the main thing. I have good memories of that period. Kevin—who would be dead in two years—and I both talked of someday becoming professional actors.

My stepfather had fantasies of me someday going to college, but I knew I sure wasn't headed in that direction. My academic interest was next to nil. My grades weren't much better. Sex, drugs, and rock and roll came first. Okay, kids, let's talk a little about the sex.

I reached puberty pretty early. By eleven or twelve I had matured sexually and had an incredible appetite for it. That's all I could think about. I'd walk around with a hard-on all day long. At thirteen all I did was play with myself. That's all I can remember—thinking about getting laid, getting blown. Sex, glorious sex.

My friends and I were all well aware of our bodies changing, our appendages growing, our power and manhood. We got in touch with it—and baby, did we touch it a lot. I think that we constantly have to keep reassuring ourselves that we are men. That's probably one reason I bucked authority so much, throughout my teenage years.

As an adolescent, my sex drive was huge. I can't imagine what it was like to be around me because I wanted to touch every girl I saw.

I was always curious about sex. My earliest experiences—going back to when I was as young as nine—were feeling up a friend's older sister. By the time I was twelve and thirteen I'd be making out with fifteen-year-olds, who were thrilled that I was thrilled by them because they had big breasts. I was like their toy. I came close—but I didn't actually have sexual intercourse until I was thirteen. There was a girl who lived down the street from a pal of mine, Gary, in Bel Air; her name was Pam. Sometimes my friends and I would spend the night at Gary's house.

One night we all went down the street to see this girl, who was a year or two older. There were six of us. We snuck up to a loft in her garage and asked her to take her clothes off and she did. I was in awe. For thirteen-year-old boys, seeing this girl's tits was the biggest deal in the world. You know, we must have spent hours feeling her tits. It could have turned into a gang bang but all of us were too chicken. Also, I didn't want to fuck her in front of every-body else. In fact, I was already a little self-conscious; I felt weird feeling her up in front of everybody. I wanted them all to split so I could spend time with her by myself. Which I soon managed to do. I called her up, so I could see her one weekend night by myself. And that was the first time I ever had sex.

Pam wasn't her real name. The last thing I'd ever want is to have somebody's daughter read this and say, "Mom, you were David Cassidy's first fuck!" I'm sure she's a very well-balanced person today, but because she got naked for us and let us feel her up, us thirteen-year-old boys used to call her a nymphomaniac. Privately I thought she was great because she was so damn willing. *God!* I'd think. *Why couldn't all my girlfriends be like that? Why couldn't all of them just let me have them? Why not?* It seemed so right. Once I started having sex, I pretty much lost whatever interest I'd had in playing basketball and baseball.

I fell for a junior high school student named Laurie, who I still in some way carry a torch for. But she eventually went for an older guy and broke my heart. So I thought, *Well, parents—adults—don't stay together. Why should I?* I spent my life going through these short relationships—falling in love with one girl for a spell; then, a little while later, I'd just lose interest.

In high school I had a new girlfriend every month or two. I'd just keep my eyes open to all these different girls. I can't imagine what it must be like for teens today, because we didn't even have the fear of getting a venereal disease back then, much less AIDS. No one worried. No one thought about it. Everyone just went out and did it. Sex was the best thing in the world.

This was our code: we got high, smoked pot, and went to drive-in movies because it was the place you could get away from your parents and have sex. God, I loved that. Having sex in a car— still to this day, I think it's one of the hottest things. You'd wait all week in school and dream about what it was going to be like. It got really interesting when it was a double date, when you and your buddy and your girlfriends would all be in the same car together. Back in 1966, '67, drive-in theaters were like brothels. Everybody was fucking everywhere. You'd drive in, put the box in the car, eat popcorn for five minutes, and then bang, you'd be doin' the pop 'n' gobble.

Eventually I told my mom, "Look, I'd like to bring a girl over. Would you mind? I'd like to take her up to my room."

My mom kind of turned a blind eye and said, "Okay, you can bring girls to your room, but I don't want you having intercourse."

"Oh, we would never do that," I assured Mom. Well, of course, the girl and I would be humping within five minutes of hitting the door. I'm sure my mom knew what was going on; I'm sure she was just glad I wasn't out on the street getting into some kind of serious trouble. After all tnis was the sixties.

Our generation was proud it didn't have all the hang-ups about sex the previous generations had. The summer of 1967, when I was seventeen, was called the "summer of love." Okay. Let's say it again with reverence. There really was an awful lot of love around at that time. It was free. And it was available. I mean, it wasn't that uncommon for a woman to walk up to you at a concert or a love-in and say, "Hi. Want to fuck?" I've always liked that kind of honesty.

And in those days people's sexual appetites were greatly enhanced by the drugs. Can I give you one memorable example?

One time I took a large green capsule of this really strong LSD—I was seeing all the blood veins and pores in people's faces, really magnified. After shaking loose of some friends I'd been tripping with who were bringing me down, I went home. I called up a very attractive but boring girl with whom I'd had numerous sexual experiences. She was just one of those girls you could call up and she'd come over, get high, and have sex with you. And I had this incredible desire to fuck.

I said, "Look, can you, uh—can you come over tonight?"
She said, "Sure, when?"
I said, "How 'bout now?"
"Sure. About forty-five minutes."

Later we were rockin'. She was a natural beauty, with bushy brown hair—but an airhead. We smoked some dope, which sort of gave the LSD trip a shot in the arm. I was hallucinating vividly; my skin was turning green and purple; I thought my teeth were becoming fangs. I turned out the lights and told this girl, "Look, I want to make love to you." I guess she thought, fine. I explained I was on this intense LSD trip and she should just, like, go with the flow. Oh, baby, did we flow.

I can still recall every detail of that evening. We fucked for four or five hours. And when I was seventeen, I was never one to last for more than a couple of minutes before I'd come. I never gave a thought to the girl or if one was having an orgasm. I'd just get in there and bang, bang, bang, you know. But this night, we just keep at it. And at it. And at it. I felt like Hercules with my dick. I did not have an orgasm—and yet every moment felt like the intensity of a normal orgasm for me. The pleasure was just that great. Finally, around two in the morning, the girl began to beg me to stop, and she limped home. The next day she called me to say thanks for such an entertaining evening and said she couldn't really walk. But that four- or five-hour session was the most intense fuck I'd ever had, thanks to the LSD—and in retrospect the most enjoyable LSD trip I ever had.

Perhaps because of my physical appearance—my build was slight, my features were sort of on the delicate side, my hair was long—there were always some people who assumed I was homosexual. I clearly wasn't into any macho trip. My manner was kind of gentle, soft-spoken. At least at that time it was. And I *was* loyal to some gay friends. So there would always be some people saying of me, "I bet he's a fag."

When I was fifteen and sixteen, that kind of talk hurt me a lot. I remember overhearing a couple of friends of mine—or guys I had thought were friends of mine—snickering and saying, "Ah, David's a fag" and so on. I'd wonder, *God, why do people say that about me?* It disturbed me because I didn't really know whether I was or I wasn't. This is sort of hard to explain, because I honestly wasn't attracted to men. I hadn't slept with any men. And I was incredibly active with girls. But I guess we're all insecure when we're young. I had some thoughts about homosexuality—I'm sure we all have some thoughts, as we're growing up, finding ourselves. I knew gay guys who found me attractive. And there were these other jerks snickering that they could "tell" I must be homosexual. So I was, at times, unsure. I'd ask myself, *Well, am I? Or am I not? Could I be . . . ?* It was only when I was actually confronted with the situation—when I had a real opportunity to get into a sexual relationship with a friend of mine who was homosexual and I de-clined his invitations, and felt comfortable about that—that I real-ized, *Hey, I'm not sitting on the fence. I'm really just not into it.* And I became very secure with my own sexual identity.

But I've been told that I've been someone that homosexuals seem to have been attracted to. When I became famous, through

The Partridge Family and concert appearances and all of that, I found I had a pretty strong gay following. I kind of liked it. Gay publications ran pictures of me; I was named gay pinup of the year by one. I'd get fan letters from gay guys saying things like, "I can tell by the look in your eyes that you're one of us." A gay liberation organization in London wrote to ask me for my support. I never did anything to encourage or discourage anyone's interest. If there were guys who found me attractive and perhaps fantasized about me, I was flattered. I found it mostly amusing how much people were discussing my sexuality like it really mattered if I slept with men, women, snakes, or sheep!

In my teens I was fortunate to become good friends with Sal Mineo, who had done some television work with my stepfather. Then in his late twenties, this onetime teen star (who'd specialized in playing troubled youths) was being ill-treated by Hollywood as a has-been. A swarthy, handsome, black-haired guy, Sal had found fame in Hollywood quite early—after having been kicked out of school, I might add. (I could relate to that.) He'd been just sixteen when he got his first Oscar nomination, for his supporting role in *Rebel Without a Cause*, starring James Dean and Natalie Wood. He appeared again with Dean in *Giant*, and in such other films as *Crime in the Streets; Somebody up There Likes Me; Rock, Pretty Baby; The Gene Krupa Story*; and *Exodus*, for which he earned a second Oscar nomination. And then opportunities to work suddenly dried up. Sal Mineo—one of the kindest, most honorable people I've known—was tragically abused by the Hollywood star system, rejected by most of Hollywood as old news by the time he reached his mid-twenties. (And believe me, I can relate.) Hollywood has a way of chewing people up and then spitting them back out. In the later years of his career, Sal appeared in mostly minor films. He directed plays also—some with gay-related themes, like *Fortune and Men's Eyes* and *P.S., Your Cat Is Dead.*

I knew Sal had some girlfriends. And I knew that from time to time Sal also had guys staying at his house. I didn't care about that; I never cared which way a person went sexually. Sal was just a great friend. He was one of the most incredibly warm, gentle, sensitive, funny, and hip persons I'd ever met. He had a magnetism of his own. There always seemed to be a lot of young people around him.

Over at Sal's, we would talk about things like concerts that were coming up. Sal had a drum set, guitars, and amps that young guys would be attracted to. I remember playing guitar and drums—jamming with other guys. It was cool because we were all mostly around the same age—seventeen, eighteen years old. The idea of having a place where you could go to hang out, where no one was going to hassle you, was just what we needed.

And Sal took a genuine interest in me. Would you believe, he actually gave me the set of drums that he'd used when he'd starred in *The Gene Krupa Story*, which was some special gift to give a kid. (Years later, I passed on that drum set to my brother Patrick.)

It was at Sal's that I first met Don Johnson and Elliot Mintz. Elliot and Sal shared a place for a while in the mid-sixties. Elliot, a radio personality on the public radio station, was really into the political movement. He was a very tuned-in part of the whole sixties hippie generation, part of the sexual/social revolution, and I learned a good bit from him, too. He became close with John Lennon; through him, I would eventually meet Lennon and Yoko Ono. Elliot and I were good friends for quite a while—traveled together, got drunk together, the whole bit. At one point, in the seventies, he even said he wanted to write a biography with me. We're not friends anymore—but we'll get to that later. I haven't seen him in nearly a decade.

I also became pretty friendly with Don Johnson through Sal. Around 1968 Don was living with Sal. I'd enjoy visiting them at their place. Back then, Don was just another young, good-looking, struggling actor from the Midwest, desperate for a break. He wouldn't become a household name until he appeared on the TV series *Miami Vice*, which ran in the mid-eighties. When I first met Don, who's about a year older than I am, I was still in high school; Don was just out. He was very charming and self-centered. I liked him because he had a sense of humor and was interesting. We were contemporaries with the same goal—to make it as actors. Don was always gushingly friendly toward me, although I sometimes sensed under that friendliness a certain degree of competitiveness toward me. Perhaps everyone did with him.

I'm sure Don believed Sal could help his career, which may have been one reason Don was with Sal. I viewed Don as an opportunist. He struck me as having something of a hustler spirit about him. I had an idea that he was going to survive in Hollywood— which can be pretty rough, especially for a newcomer—no matter what it took. I've seen that syndrome a lot in Hollywood over the years. You'd be surprised at the various lengths, figuratively or literally, that people will go to be famous or successful in show business.

But Don was already a very talented actor when I first met him. I remember going to see him in one play that Sal directed, a production of *Fortune and Men's Eyes*, around 1969; he was very good in it. I had every confidence he'd make it. He had the talent.

As my mother and stepfather's marriage finally ground to an end, I aligned myself fervently with my mother. At one point in their breakup, I threatened to kill my stepfather if he hurt my mother. It wasn't a violent statement, it was emotional. What I meant was, *If you hurt my mother, you hurt me.* I remembered how I felt as a six-year-old, after my dad said that he and mom were divorced. As I grew up, I could see clearly the pain my dad had caused my mom, not just me, and I hated seeing my mom put through pain again.

My stepfather was respected in the industry. After he and my mom got divorced, he continued directing films, including *Deadly Honeymoon* and *The Car*. He eventually went on to spearhead the drive against colorizing black-and-white movies. But by the time I was eighteen, he was essentially out of my life. He was gone.

I lived with my mom in my final year of high school. (My friend Kevin—our lives were still running parallel—was living just with his mom, too; his parents had gotten divorced.) My mom wasn't happy with the way her life had worked out. She had had two failed marriages. She had given up a promising show business career to give more attention to a son who appeared to be pretty much going nowhere.

During my last year of school, my mom did some plays with the L.A. Theater Company. I auditioned for a couple of parts in the production myself. I got the parts. It gave me a chance to work, for the first time, with some professional actors, including my mom. I liked the experience.

My grades weren't quite good enough for me to graduate with my school class in June of 1968. So I went to one last session of summer school to get the credits I needed. It was important to me to actually get a high school diploma. I didn't want my mom to feel she'd raised a failure. Two weeks later I moved back to New York with my dad and Shirley to become . . . an actor!

CHAPTER 4

My father was back in my life.

Once he accepted the fact that I was determined to follow in his footsteps and make acting my profession, he tried to help me as best he knew how. He paid for my first professional photographers. He got me connected with agents, who could help find me parts to audition for. And—most significantly, over the long haul—he asked his manager, Ruth Aarons, who knew as much about the business as anyone, to give me whatever help she could. Ruth advised me initially as more of a friend than a manager per se; for the first couple years of my career she took no payment from me. If, thanks in part to her guidance, my parents together were able to make a couple of hundred thousand dollars in a year, Ruth naturally would take the 15 percent commission she'd earned. But if, as initially appeared likely, I might make a couple of thousand dollars in a year, she saw no need to take from me a few hundred dollars that I could really use. Ruth became almost like another parent to me. In fact, I got along better with her than with my father, since she wasn't carrying any of the emotional baggage.

My father decided that the best way for me to get my start in show business would be to do exactly as he had done—learn my craft in the New York theater and gradually become a respected "working actor." In this instance, I agreed wholeheartedly with my dad. He was, after all, *the* authority.

My dad always revered the world of the theater. He told me he appeared in some forty Broadway shows. He occasionally appeared in films; in 1962, for example, he'd been in *The Chapman Report* and in 1964, *FBI Code 98*. And television made fairly frequent use of his services, both in dramatic shows—in the mid-sixties he guest-starred on *I Spy, The Girl from U.N.C.L.E., The Alfred Hitchcock Hour*, and *Coronet Blue*—and in situation comedies, such as *Get Smart, The Lucy Show*, and *Bewitched*. He had a real flair for comedy, often playing vain, shallow buffoons. In the 1967–68 TV season he had a featured role (for which he received an Emmy nomination) on a CBS situation comedy, *He & She*, starring Richard Benjamin and Paula Prentiss. But he always returned to the theater—anything from summer stock to Broadway. He'd most recently been featured on Broadway in the 1964–65 success *Fade out—Fade in*, starring Carol Burnett and staged by George Abbott. Now, in the summer of 1968, he was preparing to costar with Shirley in a forthcoming Broadway musical, *Maggie Flynn*. It would be their first joint New York stage appearance since a 1957 production of *The Beggar's Opera*. In the intervening years, of course, my father had made more of a name for himself. And Shirley had won a great following, thanks to many hit films, which in recent years had included *The Courtship of Eddie's Father* (1963), *Bedtime Story* (1964), and *The Secret of My Success* (1965).

My father had rented a veritable castle, high on a hill overlooking the Hudson River in Irvington, New York, about forty-five minutes north of Manhattan. It was a stone-crafted mansion, complete with turrets, stained-glass windows, swords, and armor. There'd be plenty of room for him and Shirley, and my brothers Shaun, Patrick, and Ryan. I could live with them, rent-free—the first time I'd ever really lived with my father, stepmother, and my three brothers. In fact, there was a pool house I could use, so I could have privacy, too, if I wanted to entertain any young ladies. My father said he would help me find a part-time job and acting classes, and I could audition for roles in New York until I established myself as a working actor. It sounded almost too good to be true.

And it was.

For starters, the part-time job my father found for me was in the mail room of a textile firm in the city. At the time $1.85 an hour was the minimum wage. The boss said, "I tell you what, we're going to give you two dollars an hour." I earned $50 a week; I took home, after deductions, $38.80, which didn't do much more than cover the costs of commuting from Irvington to New York City.

The youngest person I worked with was forty-eight. The next was fifty-five, and another was seventy-four. And I was eighteen. I had to don a light blue smock and sort mail. I was lonely. I had no friends. I lived in a fantasy world. These people spent their lives there, but I just couldn't identify with them. I was a kid. They were old. I'd gaze at the breasts of this forty-eight-year-old woman and daydream, *I wonder what she must have been like when she was eighteen. I wonder if I would have liked her. . . .* The answer to that question in my mind was always yes.

I'd get up early in the morning to catch a commuter train filled with serious-looking adults from affluent Westchester County—all of these people in business suits, whose goal was to move up the corporate ladder. My whole life I'd felt different from most people somehow. And those feelings were never more intense than while riding on that train and working in that mail room. I'd tell myself, *I don't look like these people or think like these people.* I had dreams that were different from theirs. I really wasn't money-oriented (although I didn't like being broke all the time, either)—I longed for artistic success as a working actor.

And I was starting to have doubts as to whether I'd ever attain that. In my first few months in New York, I went to nearly two hundred auditions, for parts on Broadway, off Broadway, off-off-Broadway, TV commercials, everything. I didn't get one job offer. Not one. Not even for the smallest part. There'd be fifty guys competing for every part, even if the job paid no money.

I'd be so depressed, so despondent after auditioning. Each new rejection would resonate with old feelings I'd had of being so thoroughly rejected by my father, dating from when he'd walked out on me and my mom.

I made a much bigger deal out of being rejected than did the other aspiring actors I knew. I was plagued with self-doubts.

I'd think about it. I'd never had much success in school. I was considered a fuckup there. Maybe—I'd have to wonder some-times—I wasn't going to have much success in my career, or in life, either. I couldn't dull those feelings with drugs or drink; I didn't have much money for any nonessentials. (My dad, unlike my mom, wasn't the sort of person you could hit for spending money.) And even if I had the money for pot, I didn't have anyone to smoke it with. Let alone know where to get any. I didn't have any friends.

I'd wonder sometimes what guys back in California were do-ing—Kevin Hunter, Sam Hyman, Steve Ross, Sal Mineo, Don Johnson, and others. All of them, I was sure, had to be leading happier, more rewarding lives than I was. Kevin was the only one I really wrote to. His letters were always a treat. And he was such a good writer.

I did nothing but work—half the day in the mail room, the rest of the day at auditions or acting classes. I'd had to cut my hair off for my stupid part-time job. I felt totally alone. Isolated. I'd lost my identity as a part of the hip, young sixties generation.

And my father didn't seem satisfied with anything I did. He criticized everything about me, beginning with my wardrobe. If I'd wanted to attend high school dressed like a hippie, he felt that was one thing. But he was not going to have Jack Cassidy's son going around New York looking like a bum.

My total wardrobe, when I arrived in Irvington from Los Angeles, consisted of one pair of regular shoes, one pair of tennis shoes, three pairs of jeans, six shirts, and a jacket. Standard teenage fare, right?

"How can I present you to my friends, the way you're dressed?" he'd asked. "And what are you going to wear to New York?" I had to admit, that had been the last thing on my mind. My dad said it was essential I bought a good suit.

One day I told him, "Look, Dad, I've been going through the newspaper and I've found some really good buys on suits."

So my dad said, "Really?"

I said, "Yeah, and I was wondering if I could go into Manhattan with you."

He looked at the ads I'd found and declared curtly, "Look, you don't want to shop at those places. I'll take you into New York and I'll get you some nice clothes." I thought, *I'm eighteen years old and my dad is going to buy me some clothes. Wow! Great. It's about time, since he knows I'm only clearing $38.80 a week at work.*

My dad takes me to Roland Meledandri, which must have been the most expensive clothing store in New York, to his very own tailor. He picked out a couple of suits for himself and then put me in this terrific suit. He also picked out for me an overcoat, a great sports jacket, and slacks. I'm trying on outfits, the tailor is marking them, the bill is running up to like $800—a fortune in those days—and I'm thinking, *This doesn't feel like me at all. I'm a hippie.* But I know my dad is happy.

My dad put his arm around me affectionately—at times like that, I could really feel his love for me—and asked simply, "Well?"

I mean, what could I say except, "Gee, thanks—thanks a lot, Dad," as we walked out of the store.

"Oh, you don't have to thank me," he responded, "because you're going to pay for it." What??? "You're going to pay me fifteen dollars a week until you've paid it all back." Motherfucker.

That was a significant day for me; I felt like I was finally seeing my father the way my mother had long seen him: that was a dirty trick to play on his son. Like, "How much in debt can I get my son to me? I'll take him to the most expensive shop in town and make him owe it to me!"

My dad said that no one had given him money when he was young, and he expected me to do exactly what he had done. And you know what? I eventually paid him every cent back. That prick.

My relationship with my father was very strained, but I developed a good relationship with Shirley. Anyone who knows her knows it would be heard not to like her. She's a wonderful human being.

But now, when I was eighteen, my dad—who hadn't really been a part of my life at all in recent years—suddenly decided he was going to be my father. In Irvington-on-Hudson he laid down all sorts of ground rules for me that I'd never had when I lived with my mom, who always gave me a very free rein.

I'd say, "What the fuck are you talking about?" Hey! Don't use that language with me!

He'd say, "You're going to do this and that and gain some responsibility. You're going to buckle down."

He wanted to make up for all the years he hadn't been around.

Discipline. We always had a lot of friction. And heaven help me if I told him I'd done something like arrive at an audition fifteen minutes late. He'd rage, "You don't show up for an eight o'clock call at eight-fifteen! That's unprofessional!" And I'd be like, "Give me a fucking break, Dad. I'm *not* a professional. Yet. I'm eighteen years old." But he was stubborn. And I was stubborn. We were very much alike, I think.

"Very much so," Shirley says. Here's her take on the situation: "Of all the boys—and I've said this many, many times—I think David is the most like his father. Not necessarily in terms of appearance, I'm talking about all of the mannerisms, the humor, so many things that he does. All of his expressions, his little looks, his walk—the whole thing. The interesting part is that David spent the least amount of time with Jack. So it has to be genetic."

She also notes: "The truth is, Jack didn't want David to become a performer too young. Jack really was not thrilled with David's decision to go right into the business. He would have preferred it if David could have applied himself more in high school and have gone on to college." Yeah right. Like you did, Dad?

Meanwhile, Dad and Shirley went on the road for previews of *Maggie Flynn*, prior to its scheduled October 23, 1968, opening at the ANTA Theater in New York. They were out of town when I got hired for my first real professional job, in a forthcoming new Broadway musical comedy, *The Fig Leaves Are Falling*, with Barry Nelson, Dorothy Loudon, and Jenny O'Hara. It was being staged by George Abbott, the legendary octogenarian director/writer/producer, who had worked in past years with both my parents. I'd be in four scenes and get to sing two songs with Dorothy Loudon. My dad and Shirley were thrilled when I telephoned them with the news.

Then I telephoned the people I worked for part-time, out at the mail room, and declared I'd never be going back to that hated job. "Send my final check to my home—no, better yet, keep my check!" I told them. What did I need with a check for $38.80? I was being offered $175 a week—a veritable fortune—to appear in a show staged by George Abbott. In a career spanning five decades, Abbott had worked on more Broadway hits—*Pal Joey, On the Town, Pajama Game, Damn Yankees, A Funny Thing Happened on the Way to the Forum*, and countless others—than probably anyone else in the business. I could imagine *The Fig Leaves Are Falling* running for many years to come, and me collecting those huge $175 checks, week after endless week.

Ah . . . at eighteen I had a good imagination. *The Fig Leaves Are Falling* opened at Broadway's Broadhurst Theatre on January 2, 1969. It closed on January 4, 1969.

My dad and Shirley's show, *Maggie Flynn*, didn't fare all that much better. Shirley's popularity as a film star helped generate some ticket sales, but not enough. By mid-January we were all out of work. My dad and Shirley decided to return to California. He was soon playing guest roles on such TV shows as *That Girl, Matt Lincoln*, and *That's Life*. Shirley, besides doing occasional TV guest shots, was acting in motion pictures once again: *The Happy Ending* in 1969 and *The Cheyenne Social Club* in 1970.

Fortunately for me while we were doing previews in Philadelphia, a casting director from CBS films saw me and wanted me to screen-test for a movie he was casting. So two days after we closed on Broadway I was on a plane back to Hollywood to test. Ruth began managing my career for real. She really cared about me, my dad, and my stepmom. And she was an extremely loyal person. If my dad wanted her to look after me, she would—even if there wasn't any guarantee there'd be much in it for her. She helped me find a good agent and made sure the agent was sending me out to audition for appropriate parts.

For those who imagine that show business is all fun 'n' parties, where everyone is guaranteed to immediately make a huge fortune, you should consider this: if you didn't see me during the three-performance run of *The Fig Leaves Are Falling* on Broadway, you would have had no other chance to see me perform professionally in 1969 until the year was almost over. I didn't get the film role I screen-tested for, nor did I get a number of other parts I auditioned for. In the final two months of the year, I was seen on episodes of two television series, *The Survivors* on ABC and *Ironside*, which was my first television lead, on NBC. And that was it for the year. My total earnings for 1968 had been well below the poverty level. And they weren't much better for 1969. Ruth expressed great hopes for the future. So did I.

I was back living with my mom—and feeling a little too old for that. First we lived in the home we'd lived in before I'd gone to New York; then we moved into a small apartment. My mom covered up most of the cost, while I saved money. She made it clear that I'd have to become self-sufficient as soon as possible, because she'd decided she wanted to move back to West Orange. She had never really bought into the Hollywood lifestyle. And now, after two painful divorces, she really felt like returning to her roots. She felt that spending more time with my grandfather, who was eighty-one and in declining health, would be good for both him and her.

I caught up with some of my old friends, like Kevin Hunter, who wasn't having luck at all finding work acting, and Sam Hyman, who had found steady, if far from high-paying, employment as an apprentice film editor. I wasn't sure how serious Kevin was about making it as an actor. I thought that temperamentally he would have been better suited to be a writer. But we'd have fun goofing around. One night we both got on his lightweight girls'-model Honda 50 motorcycle and drove up to the Los Angeles V.A. Hospital. We scaled an eleven-foot fence and stole a a big metal tank of nitrous oxide—laughing gas. We rode double back to his place with me carrying the tank. Got high on that for a week, then one night we went back to the hospital, returned the empty tank to the room we'd taken it from, and liberated another tank for us to party with. Had we been caught, I later learned, we could have been sent to a federal penitentiary. But we never thought about the consequences of our actions. We didn't actually steal it. We just borrowed it for a week. We did return them, empty.

I started seeing Don Johnson again from time to time, too, once I was back in Los Angeles. (Sal Mineo was in London for a spell directing a play.) Don and I would often wind up seeking the same parts. Sometimes we'd both get shot down. But a couple of times, it came down to a choice between Don and me, and I was chosen. He was always really nice to me about it—this affable, Missouri-born fellow telling me as a friend he was happy that if he didn't get the part, I did. I have to believe he must have resented at least a little that I was getting jobs he wanted—I certainly would have felt that way—but he was always decent about it. Don and I saw each other for the next few years around Hollywood; he was having a hard time getting work back then.

I wound up seeing Elliot Mintz a little, too. For a while we even wound up living right across the street from each other in Laurel Canyon. He was more interested in the struggle for political change than I was. I'd sort of become disillusioned with politics when Richard Nixon was elected President in 1968. I couldn't believe people couldn't see through Nixon's act. (I felt the same way later, when Reagan was elected.) I was more concerned about building a career for myself, and a life.

When things start to happen for you in television, they can happen very quickly. The casting directors know about you, and the next thing you know you're working a lot. That began happening for me. In 1970 I appeared on episodes of a half dozen network series. You could have seen me acting on *The F.B.I.* (the episode called

"The Fatal Imposter," airing January 4, 1970, on ABC); *Marcus Welby, M.D.* ("Fun and Games and Michael Ambrose," January 13, 1970, ABC); *Adam-12* ("A Rare Occasion," February 14, 1970, NBC); *Bonanza* ("The Law and Billy Burgess," February 15, 1970, NBC); *Medical Center* ("His Brother's Keeper," April 1, 1970, CBS); and *Mod Squad* ("The Loser," April 7, 1970, ABC).

I was gaining experience quickly. My acting was lame on my first couple of shows. But I was really pleased with the job I did on *Marcus Welby*, playing a diabetic youth who wouldn't take his insulin as a way to punish his father. I had to do some highly emotional stuff. Ruth said it was a great piece of work and would help me get more. And that sounded good to me. So long as I could make enough money to live simply, I'd be happy.

Sam Hyman and I used to enjoy driving up to Laurel Canyon. We decided to get a little home for ourselves up there. Because of his apprentice film-editing job and my assorted TV acting jobs, we had enough money to make a down payment on a home. My income was unsteady, but we knew we could carry the house for at least the next three months. We just crossed our fingers that I'd keep getting enough guest shots on television to cover our bills beyond that point. Because I was making more money than Sam, I offered to pay about two-thirds. Our monthly payments were $315; I paid around $200 and he paid the rest. Sam and I were good friends. We're still friends. When I became famous, he went all around the world with me; he went through that whole period of time with me. Although we rarely see each other now, he's still one of the only people I really can look at, talk to, and trust.

Back in that first home, in Laurel Canyon, we lived like hippies. No furniture to speak of. I found an old mattress someone had discarded, in back of a Von's Supermarket, and carted it home. We had no money in our pockets, but we were in great spirits, nonetheless. We were the most successful guys from our high school years—

the only ones who had made it and were living independent from our parents.

And we considered Laurel Canyon the hippest place in town. Bohemian Rhapsody. It was just very cool there—still very much the spirit of the sixties. Hippies next door, acid rock everywhere you went. My neighbor next door had the biggest tits. She used to just wear this T-shirt, walk around half-naked every day with the T-shirt flying. She was gorgeous. I used to think, *This is the life. Sexual freedom in Laurel Canyon.*

In mid-1970, with only eight scattered network TV appearances to my credit, I was hardly someone the average American would have known. I was just one of a thousand faces on the tube. But I could take pride—and figured my dad could also take pride—in the fact that I was becoming, like him, a reliable working actor. My career seemed to be on the upswing. And—at least as important—I was totally satisfied with my life outside of work. What more could I possibly ask for?

If anyone had told me, in mid-1970, that by year's end I'd be a household word, a best-selling recording artist, the number-one *teen idol*, with my picture on the back of Rice Krispies, I would have asked him if the acid had kicked in yet!

CHAPTER 5

"Listen, David. Don't start."

I can hear Ruth Aarons' voice now, silencing me when I tried to say I wasn't too interested in a proposed situation comedy being developed over at Screen Gems, the television subsidiary of Columbia Pictures, that she wanted me to audition for. It was something about a widow and her five kids who had a rock band. It sounded contrived. She said, "By next year you'll be asking me if I think two swimming pools in the backyard is a little much."

I'd known Ruth since I was a young boy. She was really part of my family. A complex person, she was bright, well-read, witty, and extremely loyal to people. She also impressed me as lonely and vulnerable. I never wanted to disappoint her. I really loved this woman. And wanted her to be proud of me.

At age nineteen I did not see that Ruth could also be manipulative. Everyone Ruth represented became very successful—they won Oscar and Tony awards; they made lots of money. Many other aspiring young actors in Hollywood would have died to have someone as savvy as Ruth Aarons take an interest in them. And I certainly respected her judgment. Still, I could not quite understand why she seemed to be pushing me toward this fluffy-sounding sitcom. My instincts told me I should be doing more sophisticated work; my television appearances to date had all been on dramatic shows. No comedy. No music. I was building up a reputation with casting directors as a serious young actor. Ruth wanted me to try out for this show. She never mentioned to me who else might be trying out for a role in it.

I read for the part a couple of times. I went into Screen Gems and met Renee Valente, who headed casting; Paul Witt, one of the show's producers, who was just beginning his career; and Bernard Slade, the writer of the pilot, who'd created a lot of the studio's TV half hours, like *The Flying Nun* and *Love on a Rooftop*. He later would write the hit Broadway plays *Same Time, Next Year* and *Tribute*. They felt this could become a popular, family-oriented show. They said it was about a rock group; Screen Gems, they noted, had had considerable success in this field with the Monkees. When they mentioned rock, I started telling them about Jimi Hendrix and Eric Clapton, where my musical tastes were, as if that really mattered to them.

But the scenes they had me read seemed awfully thin. I had lines like: "Gee, Mom . . ." and "Can I borrow the keys to the bus?" I said, "This really doesn't seem like any kind of a part for me." Their position was: "Well, you're not a big star; what do you want?" I said, "I want to be an actor, eventually in the movies. I want to be deep and real and serious. I've already done some weighty roles on TV. On *Bonanza* I played a killer."

I told Ruth I wasn't interested in the show. I knew from my

father that turning down the wrong roles is very important for an actor's career. My father had turned down plenty of roles he didn't feel were quite right, and rarely ever regretted his decisions. In fact, he'd just turned down a role that was actually written with him in mind—a vain, shallow, buffoon-like newsman on a proposed sitcom starring Mary Tyler Moore. Ruth said that as a newcomer in Hollywood, I was not in a position to turn down any potential opportunities for work. And there was that dark cloud hanging over my head called "the rent, boy!"

She convinced me to do a screen test on the following Monday morning. And who was the first person I saw there? Shirley Jones. Genuinely puzzled, I looked at her and asked, "What are you doing here?"

"I'm playing your mother!" she told me. And I nearly fell over. She explained that she'd been talking to them about this role—the lead in the proposed sitcom—for weeks. And the night before, she'd been told that the producers had in fact chosen her for it. Ruth Aarons, who was, of course, Shirley's manager as well as mine, had told Shirley that I was auditioning for the role of Shirley's son, but hadn't told me anything at all about Shirley's involvement. I was happy to find Shirley there; I really liked her and always respected her acting ability.

That same morning I also met Susan Dey, who would be playing my sister Laurie on the show. She was fifteen then, a teenage model who'd appeared in *Seventeen* magazine. Her skin was almost translucent. Very beautiful. Very skinny. Very naive. And seemed, somehow, very alive. She'd never been to California before. She lived in a little town in upstate New York, Mount Kisco. I remember the first time we did a scene: when they said they were going to do a close-up, she came over to me and said (I later reminded her about this many times, which irked her to no end), "What's a close-up?"

Because we were close in age—she was almost sixteen and I was nineteen—we instantly got along. There was definitely a physical attraction, too. But because of her sweetness and her naivete and the fact that she was fifteen, I just couldn't take advantage of her. Well, to be honest, she also had her agent with her, to chaperon her. We went on a couple of dinner dates, but it was always the three of us—her agent watching me like a hawk. Susan and I became friends. I didn't really date girls who were that young, anyway; I dated girls ranging in age from about nineteen to twenty-six.

Susan and I hung out a lot, though. Susan confided in me about her life, I confided in her about mine. We came to know each other really well. I met her family. I came to find out much later she had a pretty distressing background. She always had depth, a kind of soul, which is why I think I always liked Susan. There was a song that was out by the Buckinghams in '66 that I really felt was cool, with a line, "Susan, looks like I'm losin'. I'm losin' my mind." So every time I would call her, for many years, I'd start with singing that line.

We filmed *The Partridge Family* pilot in Los Angeles and Las Vegas. I remember they showed us the outfits they had designed for us—these velvet suits and shit. And I looked at this velvet and thought, *I wouldn't fucking wear this*. I mean, I was a guy who lived like a hippie in Laurel Canyon. But I put on these supposedly hip costumes like they asked me to; I told myself the pilot would probably never lead to anything, anyway. In Hollywood, you know, they shoot countless pilots that never actually become TV series.

The pilot was called "The Family Business." In it, Shirley Jones, playing a widow, hears a racket in the garage one day. It's her five wholesome but high-spirited kids, who are forming a band. The kids decide that Mom's soprano voice is just what they need, and they decide to add her to their band. (The story was inspired by the Cowsills, a family group consisting of a mother and her six children, which in 1967 and '68 recorded such hits as "Indian

Lake," "Poor Baby," and "The Rain, the Park, and Other Things.")
The family then tape-records a number. The smart-alecky middle
son (played by Danny Bonaduce) forces a hapless agent (Dave Madden) to listen to their music by shoving a tape recorder under a
bathroom stall. The agent then books the family into Las Vegas.
They drive there in a bus that they've painted in psychedelic colors,
don their stunning velvet suits, and—after uplifting words from
Mom to get them over their stage fright—proceed to wow the
crowd. Everyone loves their music. They're a hit. The proposed
series was expected to track the family's adventures in show business,
as well as the kids' antics offstage. For me, the biggest thrill of
making the pilot was seeing Las Vegas for the first time in my life,
although I was bummed out that they wouldn't let me in the
casinos; at nineteen I was too young.

Even if the series ever became a reality, I didn't see how it
could do much for me. After all, I wasn't the star of it—Shirley
had top billing; I was just one of the kids. And in scenes with six
of us around the dinner table, I figured we'd each get a line or two.
After the various dramatic guest shots I'd done, the part seemed
like a real comedown. I mean, how much could an actor do with a
line like, "Hi, Mom, I'm home from school"? Or "Please pass the
milk"? But we soon got word that ABC had decided to buy the
show. It would air Friday nights at 8:30. Screen Gems didn't offer
me a great deal of money for doing it—just $600 a week—but I
accepted that; I heard they didn't pay anyone much money. (Three
years earlier they had hired the Monkees for $400 a week apiece.) I
figured I'd have steady work for a while. Even if the series just lasted
thirteen weeks, it would mean I'd be able to hold on to the house
Sam and I had.

If the *Partridge Family* show clicked, I'd be contractually obli-
gated to do it for seven years—but I'd had too many disappointments to dare assume the show was going to click. This seven-year
contract also had something in there about their owning the rights

to my name, voice, likeness, and blah-blah-blah. I couldn't really imagine why they'd want rights to my name, voice, likeness, and all that. I was just some struggling unknown actor.

In the summer of 1970, after ABC had bought the pilot, things felt really fine. I had a job. I was making a good living. I had a nice house—particularly for someone who was barely twenty years old. My career was just about to break. It was kind of all set up for me. ABC was beginning to crank up the publicity machine. Although I hadn't yet filtered into the mainstream of America, my face was starting to appear in teen magazines.

Sam Hyman and Steve Ross, my old friend from garage-band days, planned a day for us all to hang out and get back to nature, up at Tuna Canyon. Steve arrived at the house around 5 A.M. with a couple of girls he knew. They brought peyote buttons and we all took this peyote, drinking it in blended shakes that tasted awful, really nauseating. In fact, I threw up in Venice, before we got to Tuna Canyon. We drove out there in my 1968 Mustang. At the time there was nothing around the canyon—maybe four homes. The area was a wilderness. We parked on Tuna Canyon Road and hiked up into the mountains. We took off our clothes, stripped down to underwear. Actually, I was in a little loincloth I'd made specifically for the occasion. I kept referring to myself as "Soaring Eagle"—saying things like, "Soaring Eagle see such-and-such" and "Soaring Eagle want to fly." Sam I called "Running Deer." Steve was "Bircher Boots"—because he was wearing these black military boots that made me think of the John Birch Society. I don't really remember what we called the girls; I addressed one of them as "you little forest creature." And she'd say things like, if her boyfriend ever found out she was spending the day with us guys, he'd kill us. Nice guy. The peyote created a wonderful natural high; it didn't feel chemical, like speed or acid. It was just an inspiring, blissful high.

We were out there for six hours, from about 8 A.M. to 2 P.M.

My nervous system was tumbling. It felt really good. It was a magnificent day, blue sky, seventy-five degrees, perfect. We'd brought a joint with us, too—some really strong pot—and we enjoyed that. The girls were with us, but there wasn't any sex going on; this wasn't an orgy. We were just all hanging together. It was completely being in tune with nature, feeling like a wild animal. We barely even noticed it when the girls left, saying they had to go find some water; their throats were parched.

In the midst of this perfect afternoon, Sam, Steve, and I are sunning ourselves, with our clothes lying on some rocks, and suddenly we hear this whirring, and this really loud, amplified voice from above us: "Dave, Sam, and Steve. Go back to the road. We are the sheriffs." We look up and there's a whirlybird. Then we started running, to escape—but how do you escape a helicopter? We're stoned. We're confused. Our mouths feel like camel dung. We haven't had any water in God knows how many hours. We can't find the girls; all we know is, they'd wandered off somewhere. One minute, we're in paradise. The next, it's like *Apocalypse Now*. The cops in those days were always hassling younger people. And this was to be the quintessential hassle.

We got our clothes together. But we're hallucinating. "Can you handle it?" Sam asks me. His eyes are saucers.

"I can handle it," I say, but I can hardly speak.

Our hearts are pounding. We hike back to the road, maybe a mile and a half. And we're hearing, "This is One Adam-12. I have three Caucasian males . . ." Cops are tearing my car apart. The girls had wandered back to it. Our car was illegally parked, we've been on private property, and the cops have already questioned the girls. The girls look scared; they're worried that we've blown it by giving our names.

Those cops were classic pigs—butch haircuts, military swagger. And to them, we were just some freaky hippie scum—the antithesis of everything they stood for. In those days there was a real line drawn. They pulled everything out of my car—the seats, the floor mats, the spare tire, my guitar. They spent hours looking for some sign of drugs, saying, "We know you've been smoking pot. We can see it in your eyes." I was shaking. All I could think of was my manager. How would I be able to explain being busted for drugs to Ruth Aarons? I was thinking that if I got busted, my whole career would fall apart. It really scared the shit out of me because I realized there was a morals clause in my contract. I could easily lose my job. Screen Gems would hire someone else to play Keith Partridge in a second. This was a lot more serious fucking-up than getting kicked out of some high school.

But the cops found no drugs in the car—nothing stronger than my bottles of aspirin and vitamins. They let us go with just a ticket. Just a mind-fuck. I was still shaking. I was in no shape to drive home. And too wired to sleep for almost two days, once I got there.

CHAPTER

6

The good folks at Screen Gems anticipated making money not just from the TV show, but from recordings, which would be released on Bell Records, an offshoot of Columbia Pictures and Screen Gems, and whatever other *Partridge Family*-related items teenagers could be persuaded to buy. The producers hoped *The Partridge Family* might prove as popular with TV viewers as *The Monkees* had been and thus generate comparable sales of albums and other merchandise. In reality, *The Partridge Family*, in terms of audience appeal and merchandising success, far surpassed *The Monkees*.

Needless to say, I didn't see any of this coming. I never dreamed how it might impact upon me. And of course, I had no aspirations—much less expectations—of becoming a recording artist. I just thought of myself as an actor when I signed to do the show. In fact, when we filmed the *Partridge Family* pilot, which included a couple of musical numbers, I didn't actually sing. Like the other cast members, I simply lip-synched to tracks that had been prerecorded by successful studio musicians and singers. As events turned out, however, those would be the only Partridge Family recordings on which I didn't sing.

Ruth Aarons was eager to have Shirley and me participate in the making of all Partridge Family records and in whatever profits they might generate. I was pretty much an unknown factor.

Ruth telephoned Wes Farrell, whom Screen Gems and Bell Records had picked to produce the Partridge Family's records. Ruth insisted, "You guys don't know this, but David's actually a very good singer. He sang on Broadway, he played in rock and roll bands in high school. He can give you just what you need."

Farrell agreed to let me demonstrate my voice. The guy who headed Bell Records could hardly have cared whether I sang or not. When I talked to him in subsequent months and years, his attitude always was: "We don't need artists. We just need good producers. *They're* the ones who create hit records." To him, a singer was just someone to be used. He always treated me with a certain contempt, and he's one of the few people from those days I still loathe. But the decision whether to use me or not was Wes Farrell's.

I had signed away to Screen Gems all rights to my name, voice, and likeness. They had turned over the recording part of the deal to Bell. And, unbeknownst to me, Bell had signed a contract with Farrell giving him long-term control of Partridge Family recordings, including the rights to produce recordings featuring any or all members of the *Partridge Family* cast. Farrell already "owned" me, if he wanted to use me, before I even met him. I was naive about the business. It was Farrell who created the Partridge Family's sound. He selected the songwriters, the songs (some of which he wrote himself), the ideas, and put the studio musicians and singers together. He had coauthored such sixties hits as "Come a Little Bit Closer," a 1964 hit for Jay and the Americans; "Hang on Sloopy," a 1965 hit for the McCoys; "Let's Lock the Door (and Throw Away the Key)," a 1965 hit for Jay and the Americans; and "Come on Down to My Boat," a 1967 hit for Every Mother's Son. He'd produced records for Johnny Maestro and the Brooklyn Bridge and the Cowsills, which is I'm sure why Larry Utall, who was the head of Bell Records, hired him. A no-brainer, right?

Farrell said I sounded great, adding, "We'll be doing a recording session in two weeks. I'll give you lyrics beforehand so you can learn them."

Among the few songs we recorded at the very first session was "I Think I Love You." When they played that back in the studio, it was the first time I'd ever heard a vocal of mine. I'd never before heard my own voice singing on tape. I was happy that Farrell was using me as the group's lead singer, and not just a group member. He had come up with songs that were real pop showcases for me. (Shirley was primarily used as a background singer; she rarely soloed. She'd overdub her parts for a whole album in a single session, after the album had been all but completed. Contractually, she had to be recorded on every track or song we did. But rarely did we mix her in.)

I was nervous. I didn't want to fuck up, or cause problems for all these pros, who had no idea who I was. We'd be rehearsing, chatting, then we'd have to get quiet to start recording. I'd hear some voice on the loudspeaker saying, "Could you ask the singer, whatever his name is—could you ask the guy to shut up?" Or we'd start to do a take and some voice would request, "Can you ask the singer not to slow down?" or "Can you ask the singer not to rush?" I was totally overwhelmed by the experience.

In a three-hour period we cut three or four sides. That's without strings or horns or background vocals, which would be added later.

(The background singers, John and Tom Bahler and Jackie Ward, were three of the most successful commercial singers in the business.) I didn't really play the guitar on the early sessions. On TV it would look like I'd be playing, but the audience would actually be hearing some top session player like Larry Carlton, Louie Shelton, or Dean Parks. As time went on, I did get to play guitar on a few *Partridge Family* tracks, but basically Farrell wanted to leave it to better, quicker players. I really only got to play guitar on a regular basis on my own records.

To give the Partridge Family a distinctive, readily recognizable instrumental sound, Farrell decided to feature the harpsichord, rather than the usual acoustic or electric piano, on our recordings. Playing the harpsichord for us was Larry Knechtel, who'd worked with Duane Eddy, the Byrds, and Phil Spector and who would soon become part of the successful band Bread. I remember him breaking up, laughing, during the harpsichord solo when we recorded "I Think I Love You." They managed to filter or edit out his laugh somehow. The bright horn leading the ensemble on the *Partridge Family* theme song, "Come on, Get Happy," belonged to none other than jazz great Shorty Rogers, who periodically contributed music to the show, as did such seasoned pros as Hugo Montenegro and George Duning. The producers finessed the issue of whether the Partridge Family actually played and sang on their recordings by running a line in the show's closing credits claiming that the Partridge Family's performances had been "augmented" by other musicians. Considering the fact that Shirley and I were the only members of the Partridge Family who participated in the recordings at all, that statement was a half-truth.

The recordings we made were intended for eventual use on the TV show, and for release on singles and/or albums, which the show would be promoting. Remember, this was the same company that had brought America the Monkees. So of course they knew exactly what was going on, from day one. But even when we began re-cording, I still didn't get it. My attitude was, *Gee, I'm going to be a rock and roll singer!* I wasn't really even listening to the songs. I was just so caught up with being among such great musicians. I was thinking, *Isn't this cool, that they're letting me be part of this.* I was naive. I hadn't done the math. For me, the penny hadn't completely dropped.

They made some test pressings of the unfinished recordings. I took these lacquer pressings over to my friend Don Johnson. We spent an evening together. I played a few songs, all excited that the producers of *The Partridge Family* were now permitting me to make records, not just act. Don was an aspiring singer, not just an actor himself. (He got his first film work that year, in the low-budget *Magic Garden of Stanley Sweetheart*; he was still really struggling as an actor.) Don seemed really happy for me—just blown away that I'd somehow parlayed my interest in music into what could be an actual recording career. Neither of us could anticipate what was actually in store for me as a singer. (Over the next couple of years, I'd continue to see Don from time to time. He and Sal went in separate directions; Don hooked up with one of Sal's ex-girlfriends, as I recall.)

Meanwhile, on the *Partridge Family* set, at the Burbank stu-dios, where we were filming the TV show, an optimistic spirit developed well before the first episode aired in the fall. Shirley later told me: "I had a very strong feeling about the show. One never knows with television, of course; it's a roll of the dice at best. But everybody had a good feeling about the show. It was new and different, even if it had been inspired by the Cowsills. We felt we had a lot of things going for it because of the humor, the music, the possibility of hit records, the possibility of David becoming a young teen idol. We were aware of all of those possibilities that all came to be.

"The music was not my cup of tea. I was used to singing Broadway music and other more legit types of things. But I figured it was aimed at a younger generation."

I didn't realize, initially, just how young the target audience the producers were aiming at seemed to be. But by the time we'd finished making the first fifteen recordings of Partridge Family songs, for me the penny had dropped. I had a pretty clear sense, finally, of just what the music for the series was going to be like, and I didn't like it. Not the lightweight, repetitious songs I was being handed. Not the far-from-challenging musical style. Not the squeaky-clean overall image.

Suddenly I realized we had a television series that was going to be on the air. People from coast to coast would see me singing these songs, and think that these songs were what I was all about. The more I thought about it, the more I felt uncomfortable. And totally out of control.

I realized Screen Gems had every intention of trying to market me as a teen idol. When they started talking about all the things they planned to do, to merchandise me and the music, I got really scared. I panicked. I thought, *I don't want to be a teen idol. I wanted to be a serious actor. I'm a serious actor now, and I want to be thought of as a serious actor tomorrow. I don't want to be a Frankie Avalon, a Fabian Forte. I don't want to be associated with people I think are lame.* I saw the first teen magazines bearing pictures of me in the Keith Partridge clothes Screen Gems had created for me, playing my guitar just as I supposedly would be doing on this eagerly awaited new TV show in the fall—and I lost it. They were beginning to craft an image of me as this innocent young singer/guitarist/songwriter. But I really was a hippie at heart.

I called my manager, Ruth Aarons, and said I wanted out. I was only twenty, and highly concerned with what other people thought about me. You know, you're just becoming a man, you're feeling like, *I want to be cool, I want to be accepted, I don't want to do cute records for young kids, because that's not cool*. I didn't want my friends to think less of me. I got into a lengthy argument with Ruth. I tried to tell her, "This isn't me." What I really wanted was to have success on my own terms. I had moved out on my own, done what I wanted to do rather than going to college like everyone else. I'd forged my own way as a struggling actor. And suddenly there's my dad, stepmother, and my manager, standing before me saying, "You've got to do it. If you don't, you'll be sued. You won't have an agent. You won't get jobs. You can forget about keeping that house on Laurel Canyon. Bye-bye, baby!"

It was at that point that I gave up and said, "Okay, I'll do what I've got to do." Naturally I wasn't thrilled about recording that type of poppy fluff material. I certainly wasn't given much chance to express myself artistically, either on the Partridge Family records or on those I began making under my own name the following year, which were produced by the same producer, for the Bell Records label. Contractually I had to do as I was told. I resent the way they took advantage of a naive twenty-year-old. As I became popular, I certainly would have liked to have some say over what and how I recorded, and what image I projected to the public. I never wanted to be a purveyor of bubblegum, teenybop music. The music I made throughout the *Partridge Family* years hardly reflected my own personal preferences.

That said, I've also got to acknowledge—as an adult looking back, almost a quarter of a century later—that I have great respect for Farrell and the others who created that music. Farrell may not have gotten a lot of recognition for his accomplishments, because he was a producer of music for young teens—bubblegum music. But I have to say, it was quality bubblegum music. It was innocent, well-crafted music aimed at a younger audience. In retrospect, I realize Farrell had a great understanding of the genre. He understood commercial viability and how to translate that into a pop song.

And Wes had a real talent for spotting talent. The songwriters he brought to *The Partridge Family* were gifted pros. On the TV show, I was supposed to be writing all of the songs, and I'm sure there were some young fans who believed that was reality, but we used the best songwriters in the field. Occasionally I did get to contribute a song myself. Tony Romeo, who wrote "I Think I Love You," had previously written some of the Cowsills' most memorable songs, including "Indian Lake" and "Poor Baby." He was one of the great lyrical and musical forces of the era—unique and very special. Russell Brown and Irwin Levine, who wrote "I Woke Up in Love This Morning," one of the biggest Partridge Family hits, also wrote such hits as "Tie a Yellow Ribbon," "Knock Three Times," and "Candida," which Tony Orlando and Dawn recorded for Bell in the early seventies. Farrell got Gerry Goffin, who'd written pop hits like "The Loco-Motion" and "Up on the Roof," to write material for the Partridge Family, too. Even Paul Anka was persuaded to do a little writing for us. I learned a lot about pop song construction, being around these people.

Wes had some problem with the way I naturally sounded. He had me double-track vocals (the way Neil Sedaka had so often done) to give my voice added pop-ness. And by altering the tape speed, he was able to raise the pitch of my voice a half-tone above what it actually was, so that on the records I sounded a little younger, lighter than in real life. I didn't catch onto that trick until we'd made a couple of albums. I think it was when we made the third album that I insisted he not do that anymore, and they stopped raising the pitch of my voice.

As the airdate for the first episode of *The Partridge Family* approached—September 25, 1970—we all felt confident the show would catch on. I was a little skeptical of how my friends would react to it, too. I'd been so busy working of late, I hadn't had a chance to hang out much with Kevin Hunter or any of my other pals. I looked forward to us all getting together sometime. Maybe we could celebrate what I hoped would be the show's success. I hoped they wouldn't think what I was doing was too lame.

I didn't know about the music—it was a little lightweight for my taste (so was the show, I have to admit)—but I thought the basic fantasy we were offering on the show was one any teen would want to buy into. Here we were, a family in which everybody got along well enough to form a band. And this band we organized in our garage was soon turning out hit records and playing on the road. What kid wouldn't want to believe in that fantasy? In fact, as soon as the show went on the air, we began getting letters from kids saying they'd been inspired to take up an instrument or form a band because of our show. Many of them went out and bought *Partridge Family* sheet music so they could play our songs, which I'm sure pleased the Columbia corporate bigwigs, since Screen Gems–Columbia Music, Inc., owned the publishing rights to all numbers the Partridge Family performed.

Our confidence was shaken somewhat by the first reviews our TV show received, however. Upon viewing the initial episode of *The Partridge Family*, in which the family formed the band and achieved its first hit record, *The Christian Science Monitor*'s Diana Loercher sniped (September 28, 1970): "The show stacks implausibility upon implausibility from the hit record to the psychedelic bus they tool around in. . . . It's all so predictable that the viewer is left with a sense of wasted time and effort, not the least of which was his own."

And two days later, *Variety*, the showbiz bible, itemized a slew of shortcomings. Their critic complained that Dave Madden "overplays unmercifully, only Miss Jones and David Cassidy look like they're singing their own roles, the songs (by Shorty Rogers and Kelly Gordon) were nondescript bubblegum tunes with no believable hit potential, and there are just too many loopholes. Even the teenage girls who now buy records will see through the flimsy premise that the 'Partridge' kids could make it in today's record market. Show's chances look slim."

We wondered if the Partridge Family records were going to be accepted, after all. The first release, "I Think I Love You," didn't seem to be moving the first few days it was out. I'm sure a lot of people believe that if a record company spends enough money on publicity and promotion and payola, it can make any record a hit. But that's not quite true. The public has to want the record. And some disc jockeys were reluctant to play "I Think I Love You" because they knew the Partridge Family was a manufactured-for-television group. I actually saw one program director turn down a hundred dollars offered to him by a record promoter to play "I Think I Love You." Not for any amount of money was he willing to give it airplay.

The record broke first in the smallest markets, not the sophisticated big cities. But before long, public demand ensured that every rock station was playing it. It made its first appearance on the *Cashbox* pop chart on September 26, 1970, and on the *Billboard* chart October 10. It enjoyed a nineteen-week run (with several weeks in the number 1 position) on both publications' charts. It turned out to be the biggest-selling record of 1970, with total sales of over 3 million in the U.S. and close to 5 million worldwide.

The *Partridge Family* TV show was a hit with the public soon enough, too. It became the most popular show Screen Gems had on the air. And I became the focus of a lot of attention. I began getting constant requests for interviews, which meant my already meager amount of free time was being further reduced. When was I supposed to be able to see my friends?

I remember one night I answered the phone and it was an old friend I hadn't spoken with in quite a while. He starts telling me something about Kevin Hunter having gone down to Westwood Village that day. And I'm remembering how, back when I was

younger and had an unlimited supply of free time, Kevin and I used
to hang out almost every day in Westwood Village. And this friend
is telling me something about Kevin buying some Tuinal from a
guy he met down there. Tuinal is a barbiturate. A sleeping pill.
I've done a Tuinal or two in my day. And this friend is saying how
you never know when you buy drugs on the street what they've
been cut with, that maybe this Tuinal had been cut with strychnine
or something. But whatever it was, he's telling me, Kevin had
overdosed. And he was dead.

I heard those words and I went numb. Echoing through my
thoughts was all of the antidrug rhetoric I'd been told for years. All
those things people had said about drugs killing you were true. I
should have known something like this was going to happen. Actually Kevin wasn't the first friend I'd lost to a drug overdose. But
this was different. Because he had been just about my best friend.

All of our old friends gathered at his funeral. Some made small
talk with me before it started, trying to say something nice about
me having a hit record. They said it didn't sound like me. It didn't
sound like my voice or my style. One said it didn't do me justice.
"Fuck that. Who gives a shit." There was the body of evidence
lying in front of us. Either put down or die, assholes.

Kevin's father was looking at us, and maybe me in particular,
and sort of glowering. He didn't say anything to me about it,
but I knew—and my friends knew, because we talked about this
afterward—he was thinking that we were to blame for Kevin's
death. He knew Kevin hadn't done anything we hadn't done, too.
I may have been some guy with a TV show and a hit record now,
some guy who was being written up here and there as a new star,
but Kevin's father knew the real me. He knew that it just as easily
could have been—and maybe *should* have been—me, rather than
his son, in that coffin.

With Kevin's death, a chapter of my life closed. Drugs had

already begun losing their fascination for me, and now I just felt like avoiding them altogether. I was so shaken by Kevin's passing. He was such a talent and a friend. I still think of him a lot.

After Kevin's funeral, I wanted to stay clear and focused on my work. I was determined not to put anything into my body I shouldn't. No cigarettes, no pot, no drugs at all if I could help it. The work was the main thing. I was just going to work very hard. Just keep running, boy. Keep running.

CHAPTER 7

I had never read the fan magazines, the teen magazines. I knew some, like *Tiger Beat*, had been around for ages. Others seemed to come and go. But I let them take all the pictures they wanted. At first it was kind of a kick to see myself on a magazine cover. And, of course, I answered all their questions: Where did I live? Where did I shop? And on and on.

That seemed fine, until I walked into the Canyon Country Store after work one night and they told me they'd been inundated with nearly a thousand fan letters addressed to me care of the store, simply because one magazine had just printed that I shopped there. And some of the letters the fans wrote me were alarming: "I'm your long-lost brother . . . ," "You were adopted; I'm your real mother . . . ," "I have to have your penis . . ." Twisted shit.

Once the show went on the air, it was becoming hard for me

to even get into the studio in the morning. In the fall of 1970 there'd routinely be forty or fifty fans crowding the entrance. Some of the more aggressive girls would bare their tits to me, some would follow me when I'd drive home after working all day. There were girls who'd spend day and night outside the studio—they'd live there, sleep there. I'd try to smile pleasantly while thinking, *Go home, do something with your life, don't stand here all day every day waiting for me.*

It quickly reached a point where it became impossible for me to go to a store. People would stop in the streets when they'd see me. I had the number-one record in the country. I was on TV, radio, magazine stands. At first, I enjoyed the sheer novelty of having fans. I was twenty years old.

The teen magazines, whipping interest in me to a pant with their articles, were also running ads telling kids to send in their money and join the official David Cassidy Fan Club. Or buy David Cassidy's love musk. Or David Cassidy love beads. There'd be pictures of me wearing a little necklace of shells I'd made—I'd strung together some shells in Hawaii one time—and suddenly countless teens would decide they had to have necklaces like that. In fact, I'm embarrassed to admit, it was I who started the pooka shell craze. Someone else—not me—made money marketing them. A whole group of these teen magazines were beating the drums, informing the youth of America that David Cassidy was now *it*, the new star they should idolize. Watch his show! Buy his records! Buy anything associated with his name or likeness!

I was flattered by all the attention. But I didn't exactly feel unworthy of it. My first reaction was simply, *Huh, well, this is interesting.* And yet underneath, I sensed problems coming.

I went to talk to one guy, Chuck Laufer, who ran a bunch of these teen magazines. His magazines were publicizing the Partridge Family in general—and me in particular—so heavily, so relentlessly,

I was growing uncomfortable. I asked Laufer if he wouldn't mind not running pictures and stories about me anymore. Maybe he could give somebody else the attention; I was sure they'd appreciate it.

He actually laughed at me. He put his feet up and went, "Ha, ha, that's good. That's funny. Sit down, kid. Ya see, we don't work that way." He wasn't running the photos and stories about me for my benefit. Or the ads for the David Cassidy fan clubs and the rest. He explained, "We paid a lot of money for rights to your name. You can either cooperate with us and we'll make it fun and enjoyable, or you can not cooperate with us and we'll do what we want to anyway, and it will be uncomfortable for all of us. And Screen Gems might see it as counterproductive. So you make the choice."

He was using his group of magazines to build me up, to fire up further interest in me, because he'd acquired certain marketing rights from Screen Gems. All of those readers of his magazines who sent in money to join the new David Cassidy Fan Club were— whether they knew it or not—putting money into his pockets, not mine. I never saw a cent. If he could help create enough interest in me to justify publishing whole new magazines devoted exclusively to me or to the Partridge Family—and he had acquired the rights to do just that—it would mean that much more income for him. If fans were willing to pay their good money for David Cassidy bubble gum or beads or anything else, that was all right by him. If kids were convinced they had to be David Cassidy fans to be "with it," he would reap the rewards. Essentially what he said to me boiled down to, "Look, David, I'm a flesh peddler. You happen to be the flavor of the month." Little did he or I know that month would last three years.

We had other talks as the hype about David Cassidy kept building. This man, I felt, was a parasite, growing rich off of public interest in me. He eventually told me, "Since I've been in the business, you are the biggest single money-earner for us. You've generated the most mail of any single person who has been in the business." He'd been through Elvis and the Beatles, and all that. The Elvis Fan Club was the biggest at one time, then the Beatles Fan Club became the biggest, and then I was the biggest. Eventually, I think, it was the Bee Gees that knocked me out.

Considering all the publicity I was getting, I'm sure a lot of people assumed I was making a bundle. But in the fall of 1970, as a star of a popular TV show, I was receiving just $600 a week—out of which, of course, my agent took 10 percent, my manager took 15 percent, and so on. That was it. (I received no advances or royalties for making the records.) I was contractually obligated to work for Screen Gems for seven years, if they opted to continue using me for all those years. The only guaranteed work I actually had at that point, though, was one half-season—thirteen episodes—of *The Partridge Family*. As public interest warranted, the show would be extended, one half-season at a time.

At the studio I certainly wasn't given star treatment. If I complained about one thing or another—and I'm sure the execs considered me "difficult"—their attitude was summed up by this remark: "You'd better get in line or we'll go out and pull another David Cassidy off the rack." They made it perfectly clear they considered me—initially, at least—just some interchangeable cog in the grand machinery that they'd built. But I knew the public was responding to *me*, to what I had to offer. I wanted to be shown a certain amount of respect.

I balked about some of the songs they wanted me to sing. I didn't think "Doesn't Somebody Want to Be Wanted" was a good song at all. And I hated the idea that they wanted me to talk—not sing—in the middle of it. That talking-over-the-music routine was old when Elvis did it on "Are You Lonesome Tonight." I said, "This is crass commercialism. It's hype. It's jive. It isn't me." Wes Farrell freaked out. "You can't do this!" he shouted. Like I had no say in what I was to perform; I was just supposed to follow orders. Hell, I'd never been good about following orders when in school. Now I was supposed to be an adult. Wasn't I to have any say about the direction of my career?

I swore to them I'd never talk on a record. I almost quit the show over the issue. They brought my manager and my agent down to the studio. It turned into a fucking nightmare. I'll never forget the conversations. They'd stop the shooting of *The Partridge Family* so my manager could talk to me. She'd insist, "David, you've got to go over and do that spoken thing." I'd say, "I'm not doing it." "Fuck that, it's the kiss of death."

Everybody got involved—the head of Bell Records, the head of Screen Gems, the head of Columbia Pictures Industries. It's like suddenly I'm some big problem to them because I don't want to do this one little thing. I'm saying, "Look, I don't believe in it, I don't think it adds anything to the record." And they're saying how many more copies they'll be able to sell if I'll talk; that was the bottom line.

They put the pressure on me until I caved. I recorded it exactly the way they dictated. Even after we finished making that record, though, I begged them not to release it. It was horrible. I was embarrassed by it. I still can't listen to that record. And Farrell used his trick of altering the tape speed to make my voice sound higher than it really was.

But the public loved it. That record wound up on the *Billboard* charts for twelve weeks, peaking at number 6. And *Cashbox*, the competing trade publication, had it on the charts for thirteen weeks, peaking at number 1. Bell sold nearly 2 million singles with it. I still get requests to sing the song today.

A sitcom with music is more complicated to film than a standard sitcom. And the presence of so many young and inexperienced actors in our cast meant the show took even longer than normal to shoot. In the beginning it would take us six or seven days to complete shooting one episode, and then the cycle would start right up again. I was glad when we seemed to find our stride and could complete an episode in five days. I imagined I'd have weekends free. Yeah, right!

If I had any free time, it soon became clear, I'd be expected to work to promote the show and the records. In the fall of 1970 I went to my first autograph-signing, in a store about an hour from L.A. Until I stepped through the door, I couldn't see that there were thousands of kids waiting for me. The screams they let out, the moment they saw me, I'll never forget. That was the first time I'd ever heard screams like that. I was stunned. I spent three hours signing autographs and only got to half of them.

My manager was impressed, too. Ruth didn't know anything about the record business or the teen-idol business; she'd had no experience with that. Her clients were all respected, established figures in the industry. None of them had ever elicited screams from fans. Ruth felt that young teens were reacting to me in a way that was unique. From those screaming fans at that first autograph-signing, she began to realize just how big my career could be. The $600 a week I was receiving for the TV show was insignificant, she concluded. She began focusing on the rock-concert business as a potentially greater moneymaker for me.

With hits like "Proud Mary" and "Bad Moon Rising," in 1970 Credence Clearwater Revival was the hottest American rock group around. One day Ruth told me, "Credence Clearwater just gave a concert that was huge—they got fifty thousand dollars for one night. I'm going to get *you* fifty thousand dollars a night." I thought, *What, was she crazy? I'd never even sung in public. And with the TV show eating up all my time, I wouldn't even have time to prepare an act.*

The first concert booking she got me—an 8,000-seat auditorium in Seattle, in October of 1970—was for $8,000. True, that wasn't $50,000 but it sounded astronomical to a guy who was making just $600 a week. I couldn't help thinking, *My only previous rock performing experience has been limited to friends' garages and rooms, jamming on the blues and numbers by Led Zeppelin, Cream, Hendrix— absolutely nothing like what I'll be expected to do now. What am I going to play?* Other bookings began pouring in, unsolicited, due to the popularity of my TV show and records. My first album was platinum in two weeks. Ruth said I could count on spending every weekend doing concerts—two a day.

Ten days before my first concert I didn't even have a band. I asked Steve Ross, my old garage-band cohort, to join me. I told him he'd have to start learning Partridge Family songs *fast*. No problem! I figured it would be great to have buddies on the road with me.

A guy named Richard Delvy, whom I'd met through Bell Records, was hired to save the day, and he became my musical director. He hired some studio musicians, including drummer Ed Green and bassist Emory Gordon—really great players—to back me up. We put together a good-sized road band, including a few horns, plus three backup singers who also could serve as a warm-up act for me, if need be: Kim Carnes, Dave Ellingson, and Brooks Hunnicut. Between the musicians, singers, a road manager, and an equipment guy, we traveled to our first concert dates with sixteen people. I thought sixteen people was a lot to carry; eventually, however, we wound up carrying some thirty people on my tours, including security guys.

I was too busy working on the TV show to work on an act. I figured we could do every number from *The Partridge Family Album* (which enjoyed a phenomenal sixty-eight-week run on the *Billboard* pop albums chart, beginning October 31, 1970). To fill out the bill, I could do songs popularized by Crosby, Stills, and Nash and Buffalo Springfield, and maybe a little blues. I figured the kids would be going, "What's that? And who cares?" because that material would be from before their time. But I really only had about an album's worth of Partridge Family material to use, so what choice did I have?

For the first date, Ruth Aarons, Wes Farrell, and seemingly everyone from the record company flew up. It was a big event. I was nervous to begin with, and it didn't help that Seattle was hit that weekend by the worst storm in ten years. For a while, we weren't even sure any planes would be flying into the area.

I remember the emcee addressing the audience, which ranged in age from about seven to seventeen (with most around thirteen), like it was some junior high school pep rally: "Ladies and gentlemen, boys and girls: Give me a D! Give me an A! Give me a V! Give me an I! Give me a D! What does that spell?" and all of these kids screamed, "DAVID!" And generally went berserk.

I bounded out on the stage and was hit with so much light, for a moment I couldn't see anything. All those kids had cameras and they all wanted pictures. It created a startling, spectacular effect for several minutes—thousands and thousands of those big old Sylvania flashbulbs popping off.

My energy was really flying. The first song was "Heartbeat." It's a song I do first now, too. A good, rockin' song—high energy, and it builds. Just three minutes long—perfect for an opener. I needn't have worried about how the kids were going to like me. They were screaming—and in some cases, fainting—before I got my first note out. I rushed through the show. Everything was going 150 miles an hour. I couldn't really hear myself, or the band. Just those screams. I felt overwhelmed by the strength of the reaction I was getting.

The voices were extremely shrill. That's the thing about that age. They're out of control with their emotions. It's insane. When they love you, they let you know it. (If they don't love you, they let you know that, too.) They never stopped screaming. I never stopped flying. That's all I remember.

I think there were some parents in the audience, but not many. It was too loud for them. The parents were out in the parking lot, waiting for it to be over. So many kids were stomping their feet to the beat, and jumping up and down, you could feel the vibrations. The hysteria hit me like a drug. My adrenaline was working overtime. I could hear from maybe five feet from me, these girls screaming at the top of their lungs, "David, fuck me!" and "I want your baby!" They began throwing stuff at me. And in a spotlight you can't see anything until it hits you.

I didn't say much more than "Thank you, thank you very much." I just raced through it, from one number to the next—in a style a lot funkier and a lot faster than on the album.

I would never ordinarily be flat or sharp when I sing. But that night my pitch was all over the place. Was I out of tune? Yes! Probably because I couldn't hear the band. Or myself.

By night's end I was hoarse, from trying to scream over the audience's screams. I was really drained; my whole body started feeling sore, because I'd expended so much energy. I gave everything I had. You know, I was skinny to begin with. But I must have lost three or four pounds every time I went out, back in those days. I still lose weight when I perform, although of course I give concerts much less frequently nowadays.

The next day I had to go to Portland and do it all over again. Ruth patted me on the back with an almost maternal pride, as if to say she knew that her boy could do it. I discovered I enjoyed performing "live" more than anything else.

The die was cast. In a matter of days, my guarantee went up from $8,000 to $10,000 to $12,500. Eventually I got as much as $25,000 and $50,000 for bookings—gigantic figures for the early seventies. At one point, after the second or third year, I was getting as much as Elvis, and in some cases, even more. I knew it, and Elvis knew it, because we had the same agents. Elvis called Sam Weisbord (who relayed this to me) and said something like, "Who's this kid stealing all my thunder? I hear he's making as much or more than I am." I eventually talked on the phone to Elvis myself, by the way. I found he had a great sense of humor.

On weekends I'd often fly out to dates in the Midwest. I remember being picked up at the airport for one Ohio date in a 1959 Cadillac hearse; I think the local mortuary owner was the only guy with fancy cars for rent. We played big auditoriums—which got bigger as time went on. I couldn't have worked any harder than I was working. Every minute of every day of my life was booked. And I wasn't even sure how much I was really making, for it was expensive carrying all of the people I carried. But money wasn't why I was doing it. I didn't know or care.

On Monday I'd get back to the *Partridge Family* set and tell Danny Bonaduce and Susan Dey how the concerts had gone. They were both popular as well—Danny, because he played such a feisty, wisecracking kid, and Susan, because she was so great-looking and idealistic—but it was a much different thing than I experienced. They didn't have the screaming fans and all of these magazines going gaga over them.

The first time they got to share in what I was experiencing came when Susan, Danny, and I flew out to Cleveland to serve as grand marshals of that city's Thanksgiving Day parade. We'd been booked as grand marshals before our TV show went on the air.

We got to downtown Cleveland and started in this parade, riding on a fire truck at the end of it. The event turned into sheer pandemonium. We had to get on our hands and knees and duck because people were trying to grab us. By the end, an estimated 60,000 to 80,000 kids were following us down the streets of Cleveland, screaming and yelling. No thought had been given to security, to how we were supposed to make our exit when the parade was over; no one had anticipated there'd be any fuss over our appearance. The kids loved Susan and Danny, too, of course. But they had David Cassidy posters. Ah, the power of television and records!

At the end, when we had to run twenty feet from this fire truck to a waiting room, it was really dangerous. People were nearly trampled.

There were actually times, during my tours, when I was afraid for my life, because I saw fans turn into a mob, and a mob can't easily be controlled. I knew the fans loved me—they didn't want to kill me—but their emotions were at fever pitch. And they all wanted a piece of me.

That parade was the first time I'd had my clothes ripped. That was the first and last time I ever went someplace without people whose job was to get me in and out safely. I think the parade was sort of a turning point for Danny. That's when he saw me as having the fame he wanted. He started really looking up to me from that time, I think. He was very young, maybe eleven or twelve, so it made an impression on him.

And the fan madness just kept escalating. It had seemed like a lot when there were forty fans crowding around the studio every morning. It grew to where there were hundreds or more. Where were all these people coming from, getting up at six in the morning just to see me? I couldn't really go anywhere in public anymore without being hassled.

I needed to get away from that situation. So I took a week off. Steve Ross and I hiked back into the forest of Big Sur by a stream. We spent three days doing absolutely nothing but getting in touch with nature, living au naturel. It was really cool, the antithesis of Hollywood. We lived off the land, bathed in a stream. For several days we were literally naked.

When it was over, we hiked back to our car and drove down

to the Big Sur Lodge, a rustic place that had no customers when we arrived that afternoon. We had beard growth, our hair was filthy. We got in the bathroom and washed the dirt and mosquito oil off our hands and faces, so we could at last sit down and have something proper to eat. Oh baby, was I ripe!

We sat in a back corner of this huge, empty cafeteria. Because of fans bothering me, I had become completely paranoid about being in public. So I sat facing the wall, reading the menu, thinking how I didn't want the waitress to notice me; I just wanted to be a regular guy. I kept my shades on even though it was dark in this joint.

Steve ordered for us. I breathed a sigh of relief at not being recognized. I turned—and saw that a camp bus was pulling up in front of the lodge: a hundred or more Girl Scouts who'd been camping that weekend.

They poured into the room and I was about to crawl through the back wall. There's no way these girls are not going to notice us. We're the only patrons. We're twenty-year-old males. These are eleven- and twelve-year-old girls, who would notice any twenty-year-old males—especially hippies with long hair, and my friend Steve was an attractive guy; any girl would have called him "cute."

I kept thinking that if I was recognized—aside from the pandemonium that would create—all of these girls would leave there thinking, and telling everyone they knew, "We saw David Cassidy in person, and he's really gross!" I was thinking, *David Cassidy simply cannot be this person. He cannot be seen like this.* I'd built up the persona of this David Cassidy guy that the public knew from TV— and now I had to protect him!

I inhaled my tuna fish sandwich as quickly as possible, facing the wall and trying to look down. It must have looked stupid. The girls kept looking in our direction, whispering and giggling because they'd spotted a couple of teenage guys.

I put my hands up to cover my face and started coughing and sneezing, "Achoo! Achoo!" I kept on sneezing as I hurried all the way from the back of the room and out the door. By the time we were safe in the car, we were laughing hysterically—so glad to have escaped with our lives. And I kept thinking, *This is insane. My whole life's becoming an insane charade. I'll never even be able to go camping again!*

The fans weren't just hanging around the studio anymore. They'd found my house. We had so many fans hanging around the place, neighbors were complaining. We'd have to move. We found a house off Sunset Plaza Drive that cost us $1,500 a month. Sam paid the same as before—around $150 a month. He couldn't afford any more. I knew he'd contribute more when he was able to. Sometimes Steve lived with us, too. He would be in and out. He'd go off for a while, to check out an Eastern religious guru or something, then he'd come back and live with us.

Somehow the fans found out about the new address pretty quickly. Some would sleep all night, just outside my gate. It became a zoo. Believe me, I did not treat people cordially if they invaded my privacy. I was extremely hostile. I had to draw the line. I had so little privacy, I needed to protect it.

CHAPTER 8

I must have played the role of Keith Partridge pretty convincingly, because everyone believed I really was that guy. Keith was a happy-go-lucky sixteen-year-old with no bigger worries in life than what girl he could get up to his favorite make-out spot, Muldoon's Point. He was carefree, relaxed, and shallow. Throughout the course of the show, he never really seemed to grow older or more mature (although by the final season, I finally persuaded the producers to let him be a college, rather than high school, student).

My own existence was hardly as carefree as Keith Partridge's. From 1970 to 1974 I worked like a machine. Here's what my schedule looked like.

Monday we'd rehearse the TV show, do a read-through and block. Tuesday through Friday we'd shoot. Most mornings, we'd come in at 7:30 (Monday they let us come in at ten). We wouldn't be finished until seven that night. Photographers were often on the set, too, shooting us for magazines while we rehearsed or filmed. During our so-called lunch breaks, I'd have to do interviews; I couldn't just relax and eat. At 7 P.M. for most of the year I'd also be off to the recording studio until about midnight, working on Partridge Family recordings, and my own. I started making records under my own name for Bell—while still making Partridge Family recordings—in 1971. Friday night or Saturday morning I'd fly to do my weekend concerts, which would keep me out of town until late Sunday night or early Monday morning, depending on where they were. So I'd often get to the *Partridge Family* set a little late. If I could steal even fifteen extra minutes of sleep, it was worth it.

Shirley Jones created an exceptionally warm atmosphere on the *Partridge Family* set. If many of us on the show came to feel we really were part of a family, it was because of the tone that Shirley had set. She's as warm and genuine in real life as she appears on TV. She was easy to get along with. Everyone revered her—not just because she was an Academy Award-winning film star, but because of her personal qualities. Even the crew on the set—and we're talking about hardened veterans who'd worked on one TV show after another—treated Shirley with obvious love and respect.

To some of the crew, I guess, I was just some punk actor who was making their life more difficult with all these screaming girls trying to get onto the sets. No one respects a kid, anyway. And I'm sure my attitude was kind of cocky. They thought I was demanding. One of them called me S.S.—*Super Star*. I can hear him now: "Certainly, S.S. . . . Yes, sir, Super Star . . . Whatever you say, Super Dave." I'd mix it up with them. I'd say to one overweight crew member things like, "Fuck you, dickhead." If he was hassling me, I just figured I was skinny, young, rich, successful—I had everything he probably wanted and knew he'd never have, and he hated my guts for that. That didn't really bother me. I knew a lot of people hated me. A lot of the critics hated me. They'd say, "Pretty face, no talent. He stinks."

I got some great reviews for the dramatic work I did before *The Partridge Family*. But as soon as I became the star of that hit sitcom, critics dismissed me. They'd say, "Look at him, he's nothing but a pop-out . . ." I took a lot of lumps. The more popular you become, the more they put you down.

I made guest appearances on other TV shows, including Dick Clark's *American Bandstand* and *The Glen Campbell Goodtime Hour*. I wasn't exactly thrilled about being invited to guest-star on a Bob Hope special—Bob Hope was someone Spiro Agnew played golf with. But we sang and kidded, traded mock insults, and the show turned out okay. I was on hand when *This Is Your Life* saluted Shirley Jones; they brought on both her real-life family (my dad, my brothers Shaun, Patrick, and Ryan, and myself) and her TV family. And my dad and I appeared together on *The Merv Griffin Show*, singing a duet on "Danny Boy." I suspect it irked him that both his wife and his son were now bigger TV stars than he ever was (and the show he had turned down doing, *The Mary Tyler Moore Show*, had become one of the biggest hits on TV). And when he did guest appearances on talk shows, he was as likely to be asked about his famous wife and son as about himself. After working so hard all his life, I think he began to resent that. And me, in fact.

Shirley told me, "Jack always said he was not envious of David's success but he was appalled at the way he got it. Jack didn't really appreciate or have any respect for the rock-star syndrome. I have a feeling that had David made it on Broadway or that kind of thing, Jack would have had a little more respect for it. Jack used to call what David was going through being 'a monkey in a cage.' That's truly the way he looked on it. He couldn't stand that whole scream-ing teen-idol thing that happened to David. He didn't have any respect for it. I think he respected David's talent, but I don't think he respected that whole image."

As my own career took off in various directions, I also found I had less and less time available to study scripts for the *Partridge Family* TV show; with concerts, guest appearances on other shows, promotional activities, recording sessions, and whatnot, my schedule was absolutely jam-packed. So I'd learn my *Partridge Family* lines when I walked into the studio for the day, during my ten or fifteen minutes in the makeup chair, if possible.

And as I became more successful, I did more and more fucking around on the *Partridge Family* set. I really had so little fun in my life anymore; I needed some outlet. I was working all the time. I would get punchy toward the end of the day. I'd say things like, "Are we rolling yet? We are? Can you see I'm picking my nose?" I was not nearly as professional as I should have been. They gave me the rope to hang myself. I'd waste a take here or there.

Shirley recalls: "A couple of times David and I had some words. David was on tour on the weekends and making the records and singing to all hours and really burning himself out. He'd be late for work on Monday morning or Tuesday morning or whenever a few times. That I was very opposed to. I felt we all had to be as professional as we could and not keep the crew waiting, not keep the director waiting, and all of that. David and I finally got that settled. That problem had to do with him going out to promote the show, too, so it wasn't just David's fault. He was burning the candle in every way."

I'd occasionally drink a little, but I steered clear of drugs throughout the *Partridge Family* years. I could not possibly have used anything heavy like cocaine and do all that I had to do back then. I tried to behave professionally. I respected professionalism.

The Partridge Family was often looked down upon, as being

merely a cute little show. But it was very well executed. Bernard
Slade, who dreamed up the show in the first place and wrote some
of the scripts, went on to become a successful playwright and
screenwriter. Producer Paul Junger Witt went on to do such hit
TV shows as *Benson, Soap, Golden Girls*, and *Blossom*. Story editor/
producer Dale McCraven, a really funny guy who had previously
worked on *The Dick Van Dyke Show*, went on to do *Mork and Mindy,
The Betty White Show*, and *Perfect Strangers*.

Mel Swope, who was initially an associate producer, and became the producer in the second season when Paul left, went on
from our show to become a producer on *Police Story*; he ended up
winning seven Emmys for that show. He also did the TV show
Fame. He's now producing features for USA television.

A pretty extraordinary group of actors came through *The Partridge Family* in supporting roles. When you watch the reruns, look
for appearances by Rob Reiner, Louis Gossett, Farrah Fawcett (she
did a walk-by with one line), Jaclyn Smith, Richard Pryor, Jodie
Foster, Ray Bolger, Richard Mulligan, John Banner, Mark Hamill,
Annette O'Toole, Pat Harrington, Harry Morgan, Noam Pitlik,
Jackie Coogan, Michael Ontkean, and Meredith Baxter.

The members of the cast of *The Partridge Family* became familiar faces to all America. Here are some of my impressions and
recollections of them. People ask me about them even today.

Dave Madden, who played the Partridge Family's bumbling
manager, Reuben Kincaid, was a very good comedic actor, and I
liked working with him. I always found him very funny-sad. There
were times I was doing a scene with him and he'd mug—his face
was like rubber. He had been on another couple of television series,
Laugh-in and *Camp Runamuck*. We had a friendship, but we didn't
become real good friends; there was definitely a generation gap
there.

Susan and I, of course, were basically contemporaries. There was a lot of hugging and kissing, but mostly how you'd kiss your sister—not overtly sexual. I really valued our friendship. She was more important to me than the partners with whom I'd had casual sex. I needed someone I could lean on and support and Susan needed the same. We would confide in one another.

Susan became very thin. She started living on carrots, and her skin turned noticeably orange. I would look at her and say, "Susan, you've got to start eating something. You've got to stop chewing carrots." I think she had what they call the "Barbie syndrome." She was desperately afraid of gaining weight.

She and story editor Dale McCraven wound up having a relationship. They lived together for over a year. He had hair down to his butt, a full beard, wore a headband and hippie clothes. He looked right out of Haight-Ashbury. Susan moved in with him. He was many years older than she was. She was eighteen by then; he must have been forty. It's interesting because both her husbands have also been many years older. So even in those early stages she looked for a father figure. She used to come and talk with me about problems she had in her relationship with Dale—the problems that might crop up in any relationship. I don't mean to suggest it was a bad relationship.

She went to Europe with Dale. When they came back, we saw she had gained all this weight. Our mouths dropped open. Oh my God, she had tits! That became the deal. "Where did Susan get those tits?" She must have gained twenty pounds. And twenty pounds on a girl like her was a lot. It was twenty pounds she needed to gain. She was so skinny before. I was happy for her. My relationship with Susan was rooted in real love and support.

The two littlest kids in *The Partridge Family* cast—Suzanne Crough, who played my sister Tracy, and Jeremy Gelbwaks, who played my brother Chris—didn't have a lot to contribute other than to be cute.

Now, Jeremy Gelbwaks was at a very bad stage in his child-hood—an obnoxious, almost hyperactive kid. He'd come to the set and run around making jet noises. He'd run over to you and like crash a jet into you. I'd say, "If you ever do that to me again, you little fucker!" He couldn't say a line. Jeremy—who had a personality conflict with every person in the cast and the produc-ers—left the show at the end of the first season. His parents moved out of the area, and that was pretty much the end of his showbiz career.

Brian Forster replaced him. I got to know Brian a little better. He had acted in commercials. Acting was in his blood; his mother, father, stepfather, and grandfather (Alan Napier, best known as the butler Alfred on TV's *Batman*) were all actors. Brian was an extro-verted kid, and I have to give him credit—he worked very hard with a drum instructor so it would look like he was actually doing the drumming when we mimed singing and playing our musical numbers on the show. Susan was terrible when it came to miming the musical numbers. Maybe that's one of the reasons she's embar-rassed to talk about *The Partridge Family* today. Danny Bonaduce, who played Danny Partridge, was supposed to play the bass; he was given a bass that was obviously way too big for him, but the producers never cared about details like that.

Danny wound up getting a lot to do on the show, because he was funny. He had a lot of personality. Incidentally, when I first met him, I never thought he was going to be funny on-screen. I had no idea. But he added a lot to the show.

Danny had a tremendous need to be accepted and liked. He had to be "on" all the time. Obviously he didn't get enough attention at home. Danny was a pretty wild kid, and his father was a pretty violent guy. His father used to beat the shit out of Danny. The producers of the show were concerned about it. No one liked his father because of the rotten way he treated Danny. Dan would come in completely disheveled in the morning. He'd look like hell, like he'd been rolled over by a truck. Far be it for me to judge parents in the way they raise their kids. But it's one thing to be strict—and it's another thing to go whacking on someone and not give them a sense of self-discipline.

Danny was really starved for love. He needed a role model. He was maybe eleven years old when we started doing the show. He started looking up to me, imitating my mannerisms. He also started having problems socializing with other kids. When we weren't filming the show, he'd go back to a regular school and he didn't fit in.

I'd come from a broken home myself—someone who had had problems growing up as a kid because I felt abandoned and unloved. I felt Danny deserved better than what he was getting. I saw him acting out his need for love. He started smoking at eleven or twelve, hanging around with all these misfits. I saw a little of myself in him. I got kicked out of high school, started smoking really early, did things that were self-destructive. I never wanted anybody to tell me what to do; whenever someone told me what to do, I'd do the opposite. Danny was the same way. He'd bring these loser friends of his to the set—fourteen, fifteen, sixteen years old. Bikers. You could practically see it tattooed on their foreheads: *seven years to life, armed robbery*. You could see it coming. But he wanted everybody to think he was cool. I could see he was going to have problems. I remember talking to Susan and Shirley about it; we were all concerned and we pulled together. There was a real closeness, a bond, between Susan, Shirley, and me. Although Danny liked being with me, he was actually closer to my younger brother Shaun's age. In fact, Shirley took Danny home, so he could spend a little time with Shaun.

Shirley comments, "Danny Bonaduce was a pain every now and then because he was the snotty little kid. And I had to settle him down every now and then. At one point, we all decided that Danny was getting a little too risqué and out of hand. So we decided in one of the scenes, we were supposed to bring a pitcher of milk and put it in front of him during a breakfast scene. We all got together and decided Susan was going to pour the pitcher of milk over Danny's head. And she did."

On the show, Danny was always trying to act older than he really was. There was a bit of that in his stage personality, too. He lost his virginity when he was just thirteen, with a young woman who'd come to the set hoping to meet me. (Lest anyone assume that's an inevitable part of being a child actor, maybe I should add that Brian Forster later told me that he remained a virgin until he was twenty-two! He and Suzanne Crough had a bit of a romance, but it never progressed beyond simple kisses, I'm told. He says he got his first French kiss, on the set of our show, from one young guest actress.)

Danny Bonaduce, like the younger kids in the *Partridge Family* cast, was absolutely terrible when it came to remembering dialogue. Dave Madden once did this scene with Danny up in a tree house, and it took them thirty-six takes. All on Danny. "I swear," Dave Madden said to me, "if Danny fucked up one more time, I would have thrown him out of the tree house."

One time Danny and I were trying to do this shot on the lot. Danny and I are supposed to pull up in front of the house in the family's bus, get out, and say, "Hey, Mom," or something that simple. Danny fucked it up two or three times. And I said, "One more time and you're out of this scene." That was like goading him into it. The fourth time he fucked up I said, "Get on this bus!" I threw him on the bus, and on impulse drove right off the Columbia lot, into Burbank.

Once I drove off, I realized I had this power, this freedom. Suddenly I was driving down the street—cars were honking and people were shouting, "Hey, there's David Cassidy and the Partridge Family bus! There's Danny Bonaduce!"

Danny, of course, was thrilled to no end that I was that bold. That defiant. It might have been one of the worst examples I could set for him—the concept of breaking a law, which when Danny became an adult, he got very good at.

CHAPTER 9

I felt my life changing rapidly. It's hard to convey how big the teen-idol phenomenon got. America's youth were being conditioned to believe that I was the hottest young actor and singing star, *the* dream guy that every girl was suddenly supposed to most desire. Sometimes it seemed ridiculous. Walking on the Paramount Pictures lot one day, I was spotted by a couple of the girls from *The Brady Bunch*. When they saw me, they dropped to their knees and screamed. It didn't matter that they were featured in a popular TV show themselves—and in fact had been so the year before, when I was just an unknown scuffling for enough work to pay the rent; to them, I was this fantasy figure from the magazine covers.

It was exciting for about the first year, to be the object of so much attention. I could feel my career building: more fan mail and more money for personal appearances. The *Partridge Family* show steadily picked up viewers as the first season wore on, and attracted even more the second season. Although we drew a family audience, we were especially popular with teens and preteens. And even if I wasn't drawing a salary commensurate with star status, the public was certainly treating me as the star of that show. In fact, by 1971–72, I had the highest Q rating (a "Q" rating reflects a performer's likability quotient) of anyone in television.

My record sales were huge. My very first record, "I Think I Love You," won the National Association of Record Merchandisers' award for being the biggest-selling single of 1970—even bigger than "Let It Be" by the Beatles, who broke up that year. In the spring of '71 Bell released "I'll Meet You Halfway," the third Top 10 Partridge Family hit single in a row. I took pride in those record sales, even if I wasn't receiving a dime in royalties. Everything was really rockin'. I felt like I'd gotten on some huge roller coaster that was still just going up, up, up—with some wild twists and drops certain to come. I knew someday they would.

The fans clustering outside the studio gates morning and night were becoming a problem for me, though. To try to avoid them, I started to go in and out by different exits; there were three or four gates I could choose from. But inevitably one or two of the fans would start following me. That became a major pain in the ass. Losing them was really hard.

So I had to start meeting someone every morning about six blocks from the studio gate. I'd leave my car there, lie down on the floor in the back of this other fellow's car, and ride in through the gate unseen. It became an incredible hassle. People snuck into the studio trying to meet me.

Security at my home became an issue, too. There were women showing up, unannounced, uninvited, at all hours. You might think this is every male's fantasy come true. (And I'm not going to claim I turned down every opportunity for fun and games that was presented to me—far from it!) But I wanted to maintain some sense of control over my space, over my life. And here, too, I just felt I was losing it. I'm basically a very private person.

If I went out to eat at a popular restaurant, it seemed like the moment I'd get some spaghetti in my mouth, some guy would be standing next to me, demanding, "Come on, come on, give me an autograph. Let me take your picture. It's for my kid." And if I didn't give fans what they asked for, sometimes they'd stomp off saying I was an asshole. I was happy to discover a couple of restaurants that would put me into a private room so I could eat without disturbance—like the Imperial Gardens in Hollywood; I went there a couple of times with John and Yoko.

At heart I was still a teenager. But I'd been given a variety of adult responsibilities. I really wasn't ready to deal with financial concerns; I'd had no education or preparation in that area. I figured my manager, Ruth Aarons, could take care of such matters for me, although the truth was, Ruth had never really been a money-oriented person herself. She'd always taken care of building her clients' careers—she was interested in the creative end. She had generally let her brother take care of money matters. However, Ruth's brother had died shortly before my own career took off. She found other people to manage her clients' money. I didn't worry much about who was handling mine—although in time it would become painfully clear I should have. I just had so many other things on my plate.

I was well aware I had become an idol for millions of people. I felt I had to be careful about where I was seen going, what I was seen doing. Could David Cassidy be seen going into this sleazy bar?

I knew I had fans who looked up to me, expected me to have answers for everything—often to a degree that I found uncomfortable. I mean, I certainly didn't have all the answers. There were people who started quoting me, emulating me. They'd say, "I read that you drink 7-Up and are a vegetarian. Is 7-Up the only thing you'll drink? Do you not eat meat at all? What exactly do you eat in the morning? Let me jot it down so I can be like you." I had enough trouble coping with the stresses of life myself, without having to be anyone else's guru. You may find this hard to believe, but I actually had fans who told me, "I do only what you do." And, "I moved to Los Angeles just so I could see you."

For the TV show and concert appearances, of course, I wore whatever shit I was told to—whether some "mod" maroon crushed-velour outfit or a skintight white jumpsuit (often made by the same guy who was making them for Elvis). Those were simply costumes, designed for public consumption. If you saw me walking around on my own time, I liked to wear jeans, a ripped T-shirt, and tennis shoes. That was the real me: a pretty gritty, earthy person. The problem is—when you wind up working eighteen hours a day to perpetuate this public thing, the real person of David Cassidy gradu-ally gets lost. He vanishes. And that's what I felt was beginning to happen to me.

It became harder for me to do some things that once were so natural, like hanging out with pals. I'd be invited to some old friend's birthday party and I'd look forward to going and relaxing— just being myself again, like in high school days. I could get sort of nostalgic for the old days. But when I'd get to the party, the whole focus would turn toward me, the "star." And I didn't need that! I'd been the focus of attention all day. I needed to be left the fuck alone. "It's *your* birthday!" I'd be saying. And, "No, I *don't* feel like getting up and singing for everybody tonight. We should all be singing 'Happy Birthday' to you." I mean, maybe it took all my energy just to get to the party that night. I just wanted to hang out, the way we used to. I didn't want to be some star performer and meet new people who treated me sort of funny.

People constantly asking me questions, wanting to talk with me because I'm a success—that could be wearing. It took so much out of me, emotionally and physically, trying to explain to people I'd meet casually that I wasn't that guy on *The Partridge Family*. New acquaintances would say they felt like they already knew me because they'd been watching me on TV and reading articles about me. But of course they didn't know me at all. Not the real David Cassidy, who as a teen had been busy taking acid, hitching around, having sex. How do you explain all this in forty-five seconds? "Hello. I'm not that guy, I'm *this* guy. I'm not really the sweet, shallow sixteen-year-old you think you know."

You nod, you say you hear them. You seem to agree with whatever it is they say. Whatever it is they imagine. It's too much trouble to fight it. You start to tune out. There were some people who assumed that because Sam Hyman and I shared a home and traveled together we were lovers. There's always going to be some talk about guys who are roommates. I never said a word to encourage or discourage that kind of speculation. You can't control what people are going to imagine. It's not worth the effort to try. People could think whatever they wanted.

There was never time for me to read any more than a fraction of the fan mail that I got. But some of it was disturbing—like letters from girls I'd never met who were carrying on lover relationships with me that existed solely in their minds. Writing things like, "David, you're going to have to stop all of this. I know you've been seeing other women. And other men. You have to remain faithful to me. And you really must send me the money I've asked for *now*, or I'll be forced to come after you." You couldn't help wondering if they really might come after you. For there always seemed to be fans underfoot.

Once, I remember being booked to play an auditorium someplace in southern New Jersey. I arrived fifteen minutes before I was supposed to go on and went into this trailer that was to serve as my dressing room. I got out of my street clothes. I'm standing there, naked, looking for a place to take a leak before putting on my stage costume, but this primitive trailer didn't have a bathroom. All I could find was a big beer cup. So I've got old Harry the Horse in one hand and this beer cup in the other. I'm directing a stream of piss into the beer cup when I hear these little squeaky, high-pitched sounds from under the vanity. For a moment I think, *What is that? Mice? Rats?* Then the laughter. I see these eyes looking at me through an opening in this vanity. It turns out that two girls have been hiding in the trailer for twenty-one hours, waiting to meet me. They've stockpiled fruit drinks and bananas under the vanity. And now they're unable to stop giggling at the sight of their idol, naked, trying to piss into a beer cup. I just lost it. I flipped out. "Get the fuck out of here!" I threw the cup of piss, shouting, "Here I am, babe! Is this what you expected?"

And I wasn't the only one being pestered by fans. In the first year that *The Partridge Family* was on the air, my mom moved back to West Orange, New Jersey, to take care of my eighty-one-year-old grandfather. He had lived quietly in that same modest house his entire adult life. My mom told me that kids were coming around, ringing the doorbell all the time, and generally driving my grandfather nuts, because they knew that that was David Cassidy's old house.

It felt like the only time I could really be me was when I was alone in my room. Sometimes I just craved being by myself. The only time I really had to myself was when I slept or took a crap. And there wasn't much time to get the sleep I needed. If I didn't get six hours—and I often didn't—I'd be irritable. I'd tour every weekend while the TV show was in production. When the show would go on hiatus, I'd tour without pause for weeks at a stretch. Filming *The Partridge Family* actually occupied about half of the weeks of the year—in the five years that the show was on the air, we filmed a total of ninety-six episodes, an average of fourteen episodes per year—so I had time for extended tours.

I didn't want my security people to be too heavy-handed in maintaining crowd control. My concerts would draw some very young kids. I always wanted my people to be really careful, really gentle with them. But even young fans could become frenzied and destructive; they could very well scratch my eyes out in attempts to touch me. We were actually more worried about the younger fans than the older ones. I had fans who were in their late teens and twenties. They wouldn't scream and go berserk the way the younger ones would—as people get older, they tend to get more control over their emotions. The older fans were often more likely to hit upon me sexually, if given an opportunity to do so. The younger fans were more likely to simply get hysterical. Their energies were less focused.

So how do you control kids thirteen, fourteen, fifteen years old? You can't slug them if they get out of line, but you can't let them run all over you, either. Some of them could be really violent. They could actually wind up killing you, if you weren't careful. So security on tours became an issue, and many meetings were held about it.

It was expensive carrying all of the people I carried on tours—musicians, security, hangers-on. (Eventually we'd even charter our own flights.) But costs hardly seemed significant at the time. The concert bookings just came pouring in, and they kept getting bigger. My agents never had to solicit bookings for me. They just answered the phones and booked me on as many dates as possible. The more I worked, the more money they made. They took their 10 percent commission on my gross earnings and were very happy. One agency eventually made $800,000 in commissions off me. (Think about it: I had to earn $8 million for them to net that

$800,000.) They didn't have to work at all to get those jobs; in almost every instance, they simply accepted offers that came in over the phone. I was a kid who didn't know any better, so I went along without questioning. I mean, $800,000 just for answering phones! The gag in the business was that I had the world's highest-paid answering service.

And I was working almost to the point of exhaustion. When I had to travel for a concert date, I'd get out of bed at the last possible minute, throw two or three things in a bag, along with my toiletries, and go. I'd take no money with me. Even when I began touring abroad, I'd carry no cash. I didn't need it, because I was never asked to pay for anything. (Ultimately, of course, I paid for all of it.)

I was glad to have Sam and Steve with me when I toured, and also with me when I was at home. (Throughout much of this period, Steve was living with Sam and me.) I trusted them implicitly. Even when things in my life were really a hassle, it helped having these two very close friends to share experiences with me. We all lived well, of course. I had no money worries then. Money seemed to be no object.

I was forced to move in 1971, because too many fans were invading the privacy of my home in the Hollywood Hills. It turned into chaos up there. I'd arrive home and find people living in my house. Or throwing a party. There'd be chicks in the pool, in the house—some of 'em naked, trying to look inviting. Sam and Steve enjoyed the fruits of my success, but we knew we needed someplace with more security.

I bought an old stone house, with a guesthouse behind it, out in Encino, on two and a half choice acres of land, near the reservoir on White Oak Avenue. There was plenty of space here for Sam, Steve, and me. The house was expensive, but thanks to all the concerts I was doing I could afford it. Michael Jackson's family lived out that way, too. Jimmy Webb lived up the street. This house had been built in 1925. At one time, I'm told, Clark Gable had kept a mistress there. In more recent years, it had belonged to Wally Moon from the Los Angeles Dodgers, and to Chad Stewart from the folk-rock duo Chad and Jeremy. It had a huge orange orchard.

Some of my belongings seemed to get lost or left behind in the moving process but I generally didn't worry much about possessions I lost. I figured most anything could be replaced. There would always be more tours to do, more money to be made. The one item I lost during the moving process that I really regretted losing was the gold record I got for "I Think I Love You." I never really coveted awards and never put any of my gold records up on display. But still, I would like to have that first one.

I loved the Encino house. It was a great crash pad for me and my friends. Rustic, really beautiful, old hardwood floors. The place had a casual kind of funk to it. No air-conditioning. In the summer we'd just throw open the windows. It felt almost like camping out. The area was still very rural back in '71. We even had sheep in the meadow above us. To get some privacy, we put up an electric gate with a buzzer, which helped for a short while, anyway. But people seemed to find out where I was living, quickly enough. So many strangers would press the buzzer, so a lot of times I'd simply disconnect it. And too many people seemed to get hold of my phone number, even though it was listed under another name. I needed peace and quiet. I gave a lot of thought to what I could do to get some.

To gain greater privacy, I assumed the alias of Jackson Snipe whenever I needed another alias. The name had always stuck with me, and it felt good using it now.

I got a telephone answering service, but I didn't tell them I was David Cassidy. To them, I was simply Mr. Jackson Snipe. Then when I'd give my telephone number to people, I'd caution them,

"Don't ask for me—you have to ask for Jackson Snipe." My friends never forgot the name. They'd call my number, which would be answered by my service. My service would then call me, saying, "Mr. Snipe, I have so-and-so on the phone." And, if it was someone I wanted to talk to, I could say, "Okay, put him through."

I also had a direct phone line at the Encino house. But I gave no one the phone number for that line except my manager. Ruth was the only person who could call me direct, without having to go through the service. Well, maybe my mom had the number, too. But no one else. I needed to be able to shut everyone out.

For the concert touring, we had things timed as tightly as possible. If we were flying anywhere within the continental U.S., my roadie would be at my house in a limo just thirty-two minutes before the flight. If we hustled we could make it to LAX in time. We'd have the radio on in the limo. I loved hearing them play my records. But I was so worn-out, I'd usually fall asleep again before the limo even made it from my house to the airport.

When I first began doing concerts, I could walk through airports like any ordinary citizen. But as the TV show grew in popularity and my own following grew, I couldn't go through the airports anymore; my presence would cause too much commotion. So it was arranged that when I flew anywhere, the police would meet me on the tarmac and escort my limo to a hotel, where I'd go in through a back entrance. In the early days, the band and I would stay at the same hotels. But eventually we found we were attracting so many fans, we had to separate; the band would go to one hotel and I would go to another, trying to maintain as low a profile as possible. Even so, fans would somehow show up at both hotels, causing problems. It finally got to a a point where some hotels simply wouldn't take me; they didn't want all the aggravation.

I had always tried not to take life too seriously, but it increasingly seemed to be getting serious. I feared I was losing myself with this whole David Cassidy thing. Weeks turned into months. I'd realize I hadn't had a moment to think, what do *I* feel like doing? Not get up and function, perform, learn your lines, do the show, do the interview, do the photo session, make the plane, get in the car, get in the helicopter/plane, get to work on time. I felt I was becoming some crazed machine.

Before the first season of *The Partridge Family* ended, my body began breaking down from overwork. When you're under stress and completely exhausted and warped and being pushed too hard, your body had to rest. It breaks down in the weakest part of you, which in my case was my gallbladder. I was one of the youngest patients these doctors said they'd ever seen—just twenty-one years old.

One Sunday night I got back from doing a concert. I felt a little funky and went right to bed. About 2:30 in the morning I woke up screaming. I passed a gallstone. The pain was so intolerable, I was jumping around. I started banging my head against the wall to knock myself out. It was forty-five minutes until the doctor got there. I had a big lump on my forehead. I'd never felt pain like that in my life. It was like nothing I've ever felt, to this day.

They knocked me out with a shot of Demerol. They put me on this diet, no spice, no fat. I was eating toast and oatmeal, just nothing. It lasted a couple of months, and I really got skinny. I never weighed much to begin with—maybe 125 pounds. I got down to 112 pounds. I was a rail.

Then, after we'd begun the second season, I had another attack, for which I had to be hospitalized. By the time they cut me open and removed my gallbladder, I'd already become jaundiced and it had affected my liver. That was really a close call. I'm very fortunate they got it out in time.

But while I was in the hospital, things got really nutty. It was on the news that I'd been hospitalized, forcing production of *The*

Partridge Family to be suspended. Fans gathered outside the hospital and down in the lobby and started to send me gifts and cards—thousands of them. Some fan broke through security and was heading toward me in intensive care when I was recovering. There was some scare—I was too out of it to understand exactly what was going on—about that fan wanting to put something into my IV. All I can tell you is, for the two weeks I was in the hospital, it was a circus. Fans, family, media. Me on Demerol. Flying. Just flying.

Six weeks after the operation I played the vast Garden State Arts Center in Holmdel, New Jersey. But I had to return to work, doing the TV show and the concerts. It was big news that I was working again. I broke the record at the Garden State Arts Center—the biggest single day's business ever done. The box-office take was huge. Running more on nerves and adrenaline than anything else, I did six shows in one weekend. When I got back home after that weekend, every muscle in my body was fucked. I felt like I got hit by a Mack truck. But I dived right into the same pace I'd had before the gallbladder operation. In some ways it was even heavier. They had me on a stupidly heavy public relations schedule, doing five or six things each day—almost as if to make up for lost time. This was while we were shooting the TV show, of course, and I'd also begun making records under my own name in addition to those under the Partridge Family name. And I was trying to regain my overall strength. I got my weight up to 114 pounds, 116 pounds. But I was still just skin and bones.

I developed a small tumor on my back. It was removed. My face began breaking out in infections, which could not always be hidden with makeup. (I suspect the infections made it even easier for some viewers to identify with me. I can imagine teens worried about their acne saying, "Look at that. Keith Partridge has pimples, too.") I was put on antibiotics, but the facial infections remained a recurring problem throughout the second, third, and fourth seasons of *The Partridge Family*. The fundamental cause of them, I'm sure, was simply stress. My body was breaking down under pressures greater than it could withstand. I felt really burned-out.

Around this time my friend Steve started fasting and becoming diet and health conscious. He started getting me interested in it, too. I figured maybe the gallstones, the tumor, the infections, were trying to tell me something. I went on a total nonfat diet. I stopped eating meat. We all started eating natural food. I hadn't taken drugs since high school really. Giving up foods that weren't good for me sort of seemed like the next logical step to take. I wanted to feel really cleansed, really pure.

I met this great girl, Kathleen, through a mutual friend, who became my housekeeper. She became instantly like my sister, instantly took care of me. "Let me give you a back rub," she'd say. It was a totally platonic relationship. I never had any sexual contact with her. We'd love and kiss and hug but no sexuality. She really looked after me.

She saw my dilemma; it was like I was riding a runaway horse. You've got to keep riding it—you can't stop or you fall off. You think of most rock stars smoking and taking drugs. I was the total opposite. I cleaned my body out, was completely pure.

In the end of '71 and beginning of '72, I took about two months off. I couldn't sustain the pace anymore. I said I had to take a break or I'd lose my mind. When you're working eighteen hours a day, seven days a week, you have to be able to let down once in a while or you'll die. I had no fun, I had no life at home. I couldn't do recreational things. And at heart, I was basically still a teenager. I was twenty-one. My dick was always hard.

So I vacationed in Italy and France, in towns where I could go unrecognized. The *Partridge Family* show hadn't reached there yet, so I could travel like a normal guy. It turned out to be a great experience for me. I read a lot, meditated a lot. I stayed at little inns. No one knew me anywhere. I love to be alone. I thoroughly enjoy my own company. It was just great. I recharged my batteries.

I reached France right before I broke there as a recording artist. I was never that big in France anyway, for some reason. It's its own market. I don't know why. Maybe because they're French.

Then I was to head to England, where the show had been airing and our first album was being released that week. My manager, Ruth Aarons, was to meet me at the airport, along with people from my record company's British office. The radio had mentioned I was coming in and there was some blip in the newspaper; the record people thought it conceivable that a hundred fans might turn up at the airport.

Flying in, I was thinking, *I've never been in London before; this is going to be great.* I wasn't thinking about being David Cassidy the "celebrity." While vacationing in Italy and France, I'd been totally out of that mind-set. I got off the plane in England. And there were all these cops and people standing around. I thought, *What's going on here?* Some official, pointing his finger at me, shouted, "Mr. Cassidy! You're the one that's caused all this!"

I said, "Excuse me? Are you talking to me?"

He said, "We can't even bring you through customs."

I asked, "What are you talking about?"

He said, "You can't go through passport control." And I certainly couldn't—there were far too many people. Thousands of fans had shown up. Over two thousand, I was told. There was no time for me to worry about getting my luggage, they said. More people had turned out at Heathrow for me than had ever turned out for the Beatles or the Jackson Five. It was insane. I hadn't even been successful there yet.

The authorities rushed me through another part of the airport that was presumably secure, but somehow somebody spotted me, and screams started. People started stampeding. They broke through barriers. The authorities urged me frantically, "Go, go, go!" Fans were screaming at the top of their lungs. We were running down steel stairs; we sounded like a herd of elephants.

Suddenly I started laughing, uncontrollably, hysterically. The cops were looking at me like I'm a fucking fruitcake. They began pushing me, saying, "You don't understand this! There are thousands of kids out there, and they're going crazy! Move! Go!"

The whole madness just hit me like a ton of bricks. I'd come to Europe to get away from all of this. The cops threw me into the back of a Daimler that was waiting out on a field. I saw Ruth. I saw Dick Leahy, the managing director of my record label, Bell, in England. And we took off with a police escort. Dick said, "Hello, David. Welcome to London."

They had me doing press interviews throughout my whole stay in England—from the moment I'd wake up each day until I went to bed. In a week I became a big national name. It was overwhelming. My album, released that week, went right to the top spot.

I stayed at the Dorchester Hotel. By the end of the week, there were 15,000 kids in front of the hotel, stopping traffic on Park Lane. It was on the news.

The unusual thing about the English fans is that they would sing. From about seven to ten every night, they'd be like serenading me, outside my hotel. For teenagers to be out alone that late, with buttons and banners, singing all my songs—it was incredible.

You couldn't get in and out of the Dorchester. Fans were getting crushed trying to push through the revolving doors. The management of the hotel was aghast. This in 1971 was an English hotel, run in a very proper, thoroughly British fashion. The idea that I was causing all this commotion was totally unacceptable.

That was the last time I would be able to stay at a London hotel for the entire 1970s. No hotel would have me after that. The next time I went to England I ended up on a yacht because no hotel would have me after what had happened on this first trip. And it got worse!

In my concert tours in the U.S. and abroad, I visited many different places, although I can't say I actually saw many of them. For security reasons, it was often necessary for me to just stay put in my hotel room when not performing. If I were to try to even walk through the hotel lobby, fans might riot. Thus I began feeling more and more removed from the band, from my friends, from the world. I became isolated.

As the tours became bigger, the more isolated I got, the lonelier I got, the more I wanted somebody's company, and the more I found myself sitting in my room watching TV while the rest of my entourage was partying.

Everything had to come to me. That was when it became a difficult issue: who to bring into the inner circle. Is this person trustworthy? What is this person's motivation?

I started to become more and more hyper and anxious about shit as things evolved. I was perpetuating something that I didn't want.

I didn't know what to do. This thing was gaining momentum weekly, daily. I was getting more famous. I was becoming less and less me and more and more this guy whom people perceived as Keith Partridge.

I no longer trusted anybody. Everyone I met wanted me for my sex, or for their alignment to me to make themselves more important, to be with someone that famous and successful. Or for money, to enhance their own personal wealth. And it became very difficult to decipher if there was anyone I could trust beyond the original guys I knew, like Sam and Steve—who I knew were around simply because I liked them and they liked me. I distanced myself from almost everyone. It took me a long time after the *Partridge Family* years to regain trust in anyone.

I had long since disliked people's reaction to me. I was embarrassed when people started screaming just because they saw me.
And the more famous and successful I became, the bigger the arenas
and the more shows I did, the more difficult it all started becoming
for me. I felt I suddenly understood—I could never conceive of a
reason before—why the Beatles had broken up, why they were
saying they never wanted to go out on the road again, regardless of
public demand. I really learned the downside of being a rock star
when *I* became the deal. No matter how pleasurable it might be for
that one hour of the day you were performing onstage, the other
twenty-three hours of the day were going to be impossible to cope
with. They were hell.

CHAPTER
10

Every twenty minutes that I could get free would be spent with women. In my dressing room, in the lot, in my car, anywhere. This was not out of boredom—this was out of having no life. I didn't have any time to have a relationship with someone or any chance to cultivate one. But so much overt sexuality was being directed at me, and I was extremely horny.

I never hit on people. I didn't have to do that, fortunately. People said things to me all the time like, "Hi. Want to fuck?" I always liked that blatantly honest approach. No bullshit, right? Ah, it makes me miss the seventies even now just a little when I think of how wild a time it was. And free; or so we thought.

Sex was just sex. It was there. It presented itself to me numerous times during the course of the day, and I could take advantage of it or not. Pick anyone. Who would you like to meet? Who would you like to sleep with? I was twenty-one years old, my dick was always hard, and they were all so willing. Yeah, I can live with this . . .

I had many sexual encounters. Did I do anything any red-blooded twenty-one-, twenty-two-, twenty-three-, twenty-four-year-old boy wouldn't have done, if given the opportunity? The most beautiful women in the world are out there, they're calling you, going, "I've got to see you. Please let me see you." And they would come up to my room.

I also happen to really love women. I think they're beautiful. I find them enchanting creatures. I find the feminine aspect of their personalities very attractive. It feels good to me. I enjoy being with them. I enjoy their attention. I enjoy giving them attention. The difference between me now and me in my early twenties is I now enjoy *giving* a lot more than I enjoy receiving. Back then, I was more self-centered. Much more selfish. More chauvinistic.

I loved that women came on to me. In the beginning there were extras who worked on the TV show and occasional actresses. Girls would start coming up to the house, too. And they'd show up at the recording studio, on the road, be all over the hotels—fans. But women. You have to remember, sometimes there would be a thousand people in the lobby, fans screaming, waiting to meet me.

On my tours there were not just underage girls but women who would follow me around in droves—flying, driving, taking buses and trains. There was a whole group of women that would follow the tour; they had our itinerary.

When I say I had sexual encounters with fans, I'm not talking about the young fans who watched the TV show; I'm talking about older, sexual-groupie fans. When some female comes up to your car, with no bra on, a shirt open to her navel, showing off her tits, and says, "Hi"—you know what's going on.

Some would say, "I've traveled miles just to see you." I'd say, "Oh, well, it's very nice to meet you. I wonder what you've come for. Just to stand in the lobby because you wanted a glimpse of me? I don't think so. Let's be honest. What you really came for is . . ." Yeah!

Or I might say, "You can see me for ten minutes. Do you want to talk to me for ten minutes? Or do you really want to have sex with me? Tell me the truth." That's a very powerful turn-on. "Just tell me the truth . . . what do you *really* want?"

I genuinely liked some of them. They were women who I got to know, talk to, spend a little time discussing what they were doing. They could tell me what they felt about me and my records, albums, concerts, whatever it was they wanted to talk about. I would listen and have a real conversation with a real person who wasn't just someone I was working with. It gave me a chance to actually be in contact with the real world through the sexuality. Then it was a matter of living up to—after we'd talked a little— their own sexual fantasy.

Fortunately I've never had sexual problems. I was comfortable with myself sexually. My father and mother were both open people for their generation, I guess coming from the theater. My dad, at times, was overtly affectionate. I had the impression he was quite a ladies' man. And his father before him, too. So maybe my fascination with the ladies was partly a genetic inheritance.

Women began to ask me, after they met me, if the rumor about my dick was true: that I happened to have been rather well endowed, they told me. My penis became sort of legendary, in an underground sort of way. My brothers call me "Donk." It's their nickname for me. One fellow even published a book on the Hollywood scene that described me as pulling down my pants, and an impressed female fan gasping, "Oh, man, oh, man. You really have been blessed with a rock-and-roll cock." Well, I don't know if I *had* been blessed with a rock-and-roll cock or not. But I decided that if I *had* it, there wasn't any point in just keeping it in the holster all the time. I'd have to let it out. And let it out I did. I also never thought I'd be writing all this private, embarrassing shit about it, either!

I mean, okay. So I had a serious sexual appetite. When I was in my early twenties to mid-twenties I was really raging. And as the pressures of my career mounted, I felt like, *If I'm not going to be able to go down the street anymore, not going to be able to go to any public places, not going to be able to live life like a normal person—at least I'm going to have sex. If people aren't going to know me as David Cassidy, fine—at least I'm going to be me in my bedroom.* There the real David Cassidy could live; and live well.

And as soon as people started to talk to me, they'd find out I was not that guy on the TV show. I had much more adult thoughts and sexual fantasies. Part of the game became: I can do anything, I can have anyone I want. I mean, come on, who wouldn't get turned on by that?

I became fascinated with women who really enjoyed the art of giving oral sex. The dialogue became the aphrodisiac. The fact that they wanted me. I felt sexually aroused by their wanting to please me, wanting to satisfy me, wanting to touch me, wanting to be intimate with me.

We'd be in my room, one-on-one. I'd say, "Tell me how you fantasize about me." I always wanted to hear them tell me. I not only wanted to hear them talk to me about me, but I really wanted to be inside their lives. I'd want to know, "How did you end up in my room? What did it take for you to go out and buy a ticket or come back to the hotel and sit and wait or chase me or chase the car I was in? What motivated you? How much do you desire this person?" This David Cassidy guy they thought I was.

In truth I knew it wasn't me they loved; they really didn't

know me. It was the image of me, this person that permeated the media. I was trying to find out, *What made you idolize this creation? Could it have been something about the real me?*

Being a guy with a very healthy sexual appetite—a male in his twenties with a libido that wouldn't stop—I was trying to realize my own fantasies. As opposed to fantasizing about beautiful chicks while masturbating three or four times a day like a lot of younger males, I got to live out my fantasies.

But for me, the act of sexual intercourse represented a serious commitment, which oral sex did not. I could indulge in the fantasy with talk and oral sex, without feeling I'd really committed myself, in terms of time or emotion. So, not always but pretty nearly always I avoided sexual intercourse in these casual encounters. I even then had to feel a real connection before I'd sleep with them.

To me, the actual act of intercourse seemed like serious business. You took off your shoes, socks, pants—which you didn't for oral sex. The girl would also have to stay for a while—oh, shit! she might even want to stay the whole night! Which was not something I usually wanted. In addition, with intercourse, you risked knocking her up. Nobody wore rubbers in those days. So I felt I had to be very careful if I actually had intercourse. (And sometimes I was. My friends and I also took antibiotics constantly—our motto was we lived on brown rice, sex, and tetracycline—which we figured would protect us from getting venereal diseases. Luckily I only got one case of gonorrhea and that was when I was in high school.) I didn't have a lot of intercourse, considering that it was available in such abundance. I still held on to this romantic concept, that intercourse should mostly be saved for more meaningful relationships. Well, okay. Maybe not *meaningful*. But at least I'd know their last name.

One of the most celebrated groupies of the era, known as Barbara the Butter Queen, came to the arena when I played Dallas. If you were a rock star—or close to one—Barbara the Butter Queen sort of went with the territory. She was a legendary groupie, notorious in the business. She sexually serviced countless rockers of the sixties and seventies. I'd heard her name in connection with Joe Cocker, the Rolling Stones, Donovan, and others. The guys in my band and crew just gasped when they heard that Barbara the Butter Queen was actually coming in to do them all. They were really shaking in anticipation. I was sort of fascinated by the groupiedom of it. I mean in the sixties and seventies you could actually become famous for doing fellatio. What a concept! I think it's preposterous now, but at the time it was a very amusing thought.

Barbara got into all the gigs she wanted to for free because she would blow all the promoters and she would blow all the guys at the gate. Everybody knew her. She would blow everybody along the way, in order to get to the rock star. So democratic of her.

When she arrived at my three-room hotel suite where we were having a party after the concert, she looked to be about twenty-seven or maybe even thirty. She was no kid. She looked tired, and spoke with a real Texas drawl. She was not a beauty; not even attractive, nor were the two younger girls—her apprentices—she brought with her. She looked us all over, the whole band and crew, and announced, "I'll take the star, the dark, hairy one, and the guitar player. My girls will divvy up the rest." She had been through all of this so many times before. She made some small talk about how she thought rock was dead, and she had seen its glory years. By this point, I was not into the situation at all. She was a joke. This wasn't gonna turn me on at all.

One of her girls decided she would take the horn section and the other would take the rhythm section, or something like that. The girls were actually very shy; they obviously hadn't had anywhere near the experience Barbara had. But some trumpet players had brought up a couple of other chicks, who were like hookers, to join in the action. By this point, Steve and Sam (the dark, hairy one) were laughing at the way some of the guys in the band—who were so horny—were looking at all these chicks like, *I've died and gone to heaven!* So grim!

Barbara picked up the phone and called room service. "This is Mr. Cassidy's suite, room whatever. Can we have a pound of butter, please?" And up came a silver tray with tubs of butter! That was her gimmick—she liked to use butter as a lubricant. I can't say it was really different from any other lubricant, except for the unmistakable smell. Okay, let's go to the movies!

Barbara and her girls went about the business of going down on everybody. I would not do anything in front of my whole entourage; I was still much too private a person for that. But I felt comfortable with Steve and Sam. Because we'd been friends for years now and were sharing a house, the three of us went in my bedroom with Barbara. She warmed some butter in her hands, while we started to undress. I wasn't into her going down on me at all. But Sam had the look of love in his eyes.

She took one look at me and said—trying to flatter me, I guess—"Oh wow, man, you've got it all over Mick Jagger." Then, before I got too cocky, she turned to Sam and said, "Oh wow, man, look at all that hair. I'm in love with you."

She brought out this butter and put it all over Sam. You know what butter smells like when it's hot? Steve and I began watching television, she was blowing Sam, and I said to Steve, "Pass the popcorn." He fell over, dropped to his knees. It was all over for us. Steve and I rolled out of the room. Barbara must have been with Sam for two hours. I finally had to kick them out. But it was hysterical. The whole place smelled like old buttered popcorn. Funky, very, very funky. I didn't care. I loved the fact that Sam got into it. He was after all my best friend. He, too, loved livin' the good life.

So Sam and I had a little party one night up at the house in Encino. We played music. A few friends of ours came by. I lived on a street called White Oak Avenue, up by the reservoir—a very quiet residential street, with pretty wealthy people around. And, for added privacy and security, I had an electric wrought-iron gate.

We were all getting pretty drunk that night, as young bucks in Hollywood do, when we heard the buzzer at the gate around midnight. Steve answered it. The rest of us listened as some girl that none of us knew, down at the gate, started talking sex to Steve over the intercom. I remember him saying, "Okay, but do you want to suck it? Tell me how you want to suck it? There are seven of us up here." We all suddenly got real quiet, then of course we started to lose it.

We were drunk, falling down laughing. Steve and I decided we'd walk down to the gate. The girl wanted to see me, of course, but by this point she felt as if she knew Steve because she'd been talking on the intercom with him. And by the time we got to the gate, she was already down on her knees, her face pressed right up between the slats of the gate. We both pulled out our willies and she did us under the stars, right through the gate.

I think back on it; and it's crazy. I must have been fucking mad! Had anybody—a stranger, a cop, *anybody*—driven down White Oak Avenue at midnight, they would have seen this girl giving blow jobs to David Cassidy and Steve Ross through the bars of my gate. We could have all wound up in jail. But once again the Good Lord shined his light . . .

I guess it's safe to say that at that time a lot of fans would have done anything for me. I'll admit I did things that I now think were degrading toward women that I'm ashamed of. Once I got them into my home or hotel room, I found I could tell them to get down on their knees and bark like a dog or act like a choo-choo train, and they'd do it gladly. I think they were happy just to get close to me. It was folly for me. But I know now how totally unconscious of their feelings I was.

I'm not sure I felt worthy of all the adulation I received as a teen idol. You're always trying to convince yourself that you really are worthy of it. But are you? Come on, no one's worthy of all that. It's just a thing that happens. There's a lot of other guys who were more handsome and talented. I can't explain it. I happened to come along in the right vehicle, at the right time. Everything was right. Oh, how wrong innocence can be.

It's bizarre but true that, once I became really famous, virtually the only real contact I had with humans was with women who'd want to have sex with me. They'd come into my inner sanctum for a little while and we'd talk. I'd talk to them about the simplest, most mundane things. They'd say, "Oh, you wouldn't care about this, I work at this job." Blah, blah, blah. But I did care. They became my last connection to the outside world. It was like, "Oh, what's it like? You sit behind a desk? Tell me what it's like," I'd say. Because I never knew that. I didn't live that kind of a life. So I'd ask, "Where do you go for fun? Do you go bowling? What do you do? What's it like when you stand in line at the bank?" In a sense, they became my connection with the real world.

On tour there'd be all these girls hanging around the hotels. The guys in the band and the roadies—guys who were there to assist me in one way or another on the tours—would pull in girls who were looking for me. Sometimes those guys would tell the girls they'd have to have sex with them first if they expected to ever meet me. That was the deal. I learned later, there were plenty of girls who were glad to comply. When you're dealing with rock and roll and with young chicks in heat with their hormones really roarin', I suppose it never changes.

On the road there was plenty of sex for every member of my entourage who wanted it. I mean, it really got stupid. I had a guy traveling with me who had only one job to do—to hand me my guitar when I needed it for one number in my concert and then to take it back from me after I'd finished that number. I can remember

Me and a friend, 1976.

Soaking up the rays.

Me and my stand-in, Jan, on the set.

In concert.

Talking to a jockey
at a Paris racetrack.

Me and some Australian fans.

Taking a break during the Australian tour.

Relaxing at home, 1976.

At Caribou, 1976.

Hawaii.

Me and an admirer.

On tour in Japan.

A typically frenzied crowd.

Behind the wheel, August, 1974.

Some of my fans in Glasgow, Scotland.

The higher they climb...

...the harder they fall!

Just a man and his horse.

In concert.

Me and Susan Dey.

Out on the range.

In concert.

A waif.

Another sellout crowd.

Me in concert, in full '70s regalia.

Me in my ever-popular embroidered overalls.

Modeling the quintessential '70s shag-cut.

When I visited the high school in my hometown of West Orange, New Jersey, the kids gave me my own football jersey.

A few fans from the high school in West Orange, displaying a locker plastered with clippings of me.

The house where I grew up at 23 Elm Street, West Orange, New Jersey.

this one huge outdoor daytime concert where I reached the point where I was supposed to do the number with the guitar. The fans were screaming and yelling, eager for me to get on with the show. I was going, "Thanks, and now for my next trick . . ." while I'm looking around frantically for the guitar. *Nothing.* Nowhere. Finally, way off to one side, I saw this guy who was supposed to be handing the guitar to me. He's on the open back end of a truck, facing in, his pants down around his knees, his white ass hanging out; he was fucking some chick from behind. I screamed over to him. I mean, he had only one job to do in this show and he couldn't even do that! Why? Because he was fucking some fan of mine—in the middle of my show! He couldn't even wait until it was over. Okay. David might have needed his guitar then, but my equipment man had his priorities. And you want to know something? I didn't fire him. Because that's how loose things were. With everybody who toured with me, the concern for them seemed to be, "How much can you get on the road?" I'd come back to my hotel suite from doing a gig and find one of my security guys naked with some chicks in the Jacuzzi; he'd told them they had to go through him if they wanted to meet David. There was a lot of that. It pissed me off when that happened. I felt taken advantage of and I hated them taking advantage of a fan's desire to get to meet me.

Sometimes it became a contest between a couple of the guys in my entourage to see how many girls they could pull for me. They thought they were impressing me or something, or somehow proving their masculinity by rounding up a lot of girls quickly. But for me, it usually felt terrible. Empty. What was I supposed to be, some sex machine servicing the groupies of the world? It was uncomfortable, feeling I had to live up to others' expectations that I be some superstud if I was a star.

I can remember one night, I just felt awful; I didn't know what to do. These guys had rounded up seven different girls. They had them waiting for me, undressed, in the outer room of my hotel suite, and they'd send them into my bedroom at ten-minute intervals. I mean, after ten minutes, one of these guys would knock on the door and order the girl, "Come out, please." And then send in the next one. Sexist. Sleaze. I hated it.

So you want to know what I did with them in my hotel bedroom that particular night, with one naked girl after another parading in to see me?

Nothing.

I mean, I was lying on the bed naked, totally prepared for sex. The girls came in to see me one at a time. Most, I have to tell you, were fairly unattractive to begin with. And whatever self-confidence they might have had when they left their homes earlier that evening to go to my concert seemed to have been stripped of them in that outer room, along with their clothes. Whatever facade they might have had of being clever or cool, baby—that was gone.

I can remember the first girl coming in, awkward and uncomfortable, standing nude at the foot of my bed saying, "Well, uh, hi. I, uh, guess you sort of know what I'm here for." Yeah. I got that. And then suddenly it hit me and I was totally turned off. I thought of my roadies out there in the other room, so proud that they could get these seven girls up here like this. Was I supposed to have sex with all of them? Was this supposed to be fun? I felt, somehow, emasculated by the whole situation. I felt like a sleaze myself.

I'm sure there are some of you out there who are reading this book who might strongly disapprove of promiscuity, who will say I "used" women. You're right. I did. But it wasn't always clear to me who was really "using" whom. I was frequently the one being pursued by fans who wanted me much more than I wanted them. I sometimes felt I was losing myself by giving myself to strangers.

Like there was this one fan, a blonde of about nineteen or

twenty, who used to wait at the TV studio gates for me, evening after evening. After a while, she must have figured out the way I often drove home, because one evening she flagged me down some distance from the studio, pleading how she'd missed her bus, she was nervous about hitchhiking, and could I please just this once give her a ride home? I recognized her from the gate at the studio, of course, and I said if I gave her a ride, I'd have to give rides to every girl who waited by the gate. But she kept pleading fervently, begging me, practically in tears until I finally agreed to give her a ride. She said she was headed in my direction, anyway. I told her I was really beat; I'd gotten no sleep the night before; this was just a lift, nothing else. She told me how she was from the East, and was an aspiring dancer. She said that when she'd first seen me on TV, she didn't know what it was about me but she knew she had to meet me. And now she was in California, and she wanted to get to know me. I told her there were a lot of people who thought they wanted to get to know me, but it simply wasn't possible for me. When it came time for me to drop her off, it took five minutes to get her out of the car because she kept saying she just wanted one kiss from me, and I kept saying, "Look, I don't even know you; I don't want to kiss you. You seem like a relatively sane human. Now just go, okay?"

After finally getting rid of her, I drove over to Western Studios in Hollywood for a long recording session. When I left the session— it was after one in the morning—that same girl was there again. I don't know how she'd known where I was, but she said she'd been waiting by the recording-studio door for several hours to see me and could I please give her a lift home.

I said, "What you're asking me is silly."

She said, "Okay, then I'll have to hitch home."

"At one-thirty in the morning? In Hollywood? You can't do that. Oh, shit."

I reluctantly let her get in my car again and asked her where she lived. It was over in a low-rent area. I started driving her home. We hadn't gone more than a couple of blocks before she began unbuttoning her shirt. I couldn't help myself now, folks; I just wanted to look at her enormous breasts. They were beautiful. I put on the brake and sat there staring for like ten seconds in disbelief. From her bucket seat, she lunged at me, over the gearshift lever. We were getting entangled. I was sweating profusely, almost peaking, you know, and thinking, *Oh my God, some cop could come along, and I'm in the middle of Fountain Avenue, jumping some groupie I've just met today.* I felt like I couldn't hold back much longer, either. But somehow I got her home first. We pulled into this big garage behind her apartment building, and there—in her parking stall in this garage—she was all over me. She sat on the gearshift knob. She sat on me. And I just, you know, I just let her do whatever she wanted. Physically I had no resistance to offer. I'd been up for forty-eight hours, I'd sung all night after filming the TV show all day. I still had on my TV makeup, which was running, because I was so sweaty.

After a few days, she began turning up at the gate again, and she wrote me letters for years, recalling that one night as if it had been a very important night in her life. I talked with her briefly once more, but I refused to give her any more rides home because I knew what would happen if I did. And the truth is, I hadn't felt good at all the day after we had had sex. I had just felt kinda used, low, and demeaned.

To tell you the truth, a lot of the times sex with strangers had become boring. I had sexual encounters with a number of women with whom there was no emotional connection, no romance. Maybe sometimes they were getting off on being close to a star, but for me it was often like masturbation, even if another person was involved.

Once, Sam brought a girl home with him who turned out to be a real nutcase—she was obsessed with me, although she lied about it. It became a rather difficult situation, because Sam thought she was in love with him, and it turned out she had a fixation about me. But she lied to him to get into our world. She used him, but he really dug her. That was fucking awful.

He met this girl on one of our tours. She was really dirty—I mean literally, dirt all over her hands—but there was something about her. You looked at her and she just reeked of sex. And Sam fell for it, big-time. I mean, she really got under his skin. He brought her around. Showed her off. Then she got drunk one night, out on the road, and started crawling into my room. Banging on my door, crying. I wasn't interested; I certainly hadn't in any way invited her. A couple of my guys grabbed her and took her downstairs. Sam couldn't look me in the eye. He tried to rationalize the situation, saying, "Well, she was drunk." He felt duped, and hurt. I couldn't blame him.

I said, "Yeah, but she *was* crawling to get into my room. That tells you something." He was really hurt by it and a little angry at me.

Some girls tried to go through the band to get to me. The guys in the band often wouldn't want to let those girls get away. And so I might not even meet them. In the end, we had a name I coined: "Squeaky Clean"—which was me—"and the Dirty All-Night Boys." (In fact, I wanted to make an album under that alias, Squeaky Clean and the Dirty All-Night Boys. Steve and I were going to do some of the stuff from our garage-band days—all that really hard, stoned-rocker stuff I loved before getting trapped into the Partridge Family bag.)

It hardly mattered that the guys in my band may have had wives or steady girlfriends back home. It's a perverse existence being out on the road. The musicians could be really great at home, but as soon as they walked through the airport metal detectors, they'd turn into animals. I'd watch their behavior go from "Bye, honey," as they'd give their wives goodbye kisses, to sitting in some hotel room filled with fans, with peanut butter on their dicks.

There were some younger fans who followed us around who made it clear they were interested in me sexually, and some were quite beautiful. But I was well aware of the difficulties Elvis and others had had, due to involvements with underage girls. And I was also concerned about the possibility of inflicting trauma on someone who was just too young. I learned how to say no gracefully.

It was not always easy turning down those temptations. I can remember one fourteen-year-old who wanted to have sex with me, but I wouldn't do it. I felt like such an old square, declining her offer. She was a virgin, and one of the most beautiful girls I've ever seen. I told her I didn't want to be the one to take her virginity. "Save it, baby. Your time will come soon."

She said, "I wasn't going to do it with anyone until I was at least sixteen, but I want to make love to you. I want to sleep with you."

I said, "You don't know how difficult this is for me to tell you, but I can't; I just can't. It's too creepy." And of course, I didn't. She wrote me a long, really lovely letter later. That was as great a temptation as I have had.

I had some male groupies, too, who'd hang around the hotel or wherever I was, waiting to see me. Some transvestites, some gay guys. I always liked seeing them. They were always all right. Amusing. If I was ever stopped by them, I always found them interesting. I never treated them any differently or thought about them any differently than any female fans who might hang around. I'd say, "Would you like an autograph," or whatever—you know. I guess many of them fantasized about sleeping with me. Who knows.

Part of the bizarreness of being a teen idol, a rock star, and a TV star is becoming the focus of people's sexual fantasies—both male and female. I used to feel flattered when I'd hear that a friend had gone into a gay bar and heard that half the guys said they'd slept with me. I thought it was funny. I've always figured it's a compliment when someone says they're attracted to you. Gay friends would say to me, "Hey, I hear you've been spending a lot of nights at the Rusty Nail," a popular nearby gay bar. Right! As if I had the energy or the time to go out to any bars after work! But there'd be that kind of gossip. There's a great line I wish I could take credit for but I think Dustin Hoffman said it first: "I knew I'd made it as a performer when I first began hearing rumors I was gay." It means you've penetrated people's sexual fantasies.

And as my fame grew, I became even more reclusive. I was barely out of my teens, being told I was some kind of demigod with a responsibility to millions of kids. I was told I had the largest fan club in history. Bigger than the Beatles, bigger than the Monkees, bigger than Elvis, bigger than all of it. You're the deal, kid. The big brass ring.

How do you respond to all of that? Well, I went into a shell. I hid myself, who I really was. I hid my sexuality. I hid my personal life. I had some fear that if people really got to know me, they wouldn't love me as much. How would they really feel about me if they really knew who I was? I wasn't this superhuman I was being built up to be.

For a couple of years during the run of *The Partridge Family*, I went to see a psychiatrist every Monday night. I wanted help in dealing with stresses that were too great for me. I was particularly bothered by my inability to form lasting friendships with women.

How was I supposed to really meet anybody? Where was there an opportunity? I couldn't go to a bar. I couldn't go to a restaurant. In my working environment, I worked with essentially the same people day after day. Occasionally there'd be a female guest star on the TV show. But what were the odds that the female guest star would be someone you really wanted to go out with? And usually they'd already be either married or involved. So the only people I really got to meet were actresses or extras on the show or people who would somehow occasionally get on the set, even though we had a closed set.

The only way that I had human contact was through my few friends, Sam and Steve and a couple of other people, but mostly through them.

But it's an uncomfortable thing to say to a friend, "Hey, pal, go find me some really attractive women I can sit and talk to. And get to know. Or even just sit and relax and rub oil all over ourselves." Yeah, right. So that became the frustration.

CHAPTER 11

On television I may have been playing a sixteen-year-old, but my fans knew I was really older. For one thing, such teen magazines as *Tiger Beat* and *Fave*, published by the Laufer Company, made a huge deal out of my birthdays. Every reader of such publications knew that I turned twenty-one on April 12, 1971, because Chuck Laufer threw a "surprise party" (translation: photo op) for me. His magazines published photo after photo of Sam Hyman, Steve Ross, and me opening presents and reading cards. One typical posed photo showed Sam "surprising" me by dumping boxes of cards from fans over my head. The caption assured everyone that I then went on to read each and every one. That sounded much better than the reality that the Laufer Company, which was licensed to handle my fan mail (and I could get as many as 25,000 letters in a week), simply burned most of it—after first recording the names and addresses so that they could be added to Laufer mailing lists. Those youngsters would then be solicited to purchase other David Cassidy and Partridge Family memorabilia from the Laufer Company, as well as to subscribe to various Laufer publications. Nice work, eh? Dare any of you ask if I got your letters?

Other birthday-party photos showed Laufer magazine editors Ann Moses and Laudy Powell giving me supplies of cashews and 7 Up (which the magazines relentlessly reminded readers was my drink of choice). Another photo showed me hoisting what could have been mistaken for a large glass of champagne if you didn't read the caption, supposedly my own words: "Time out for cake and 7 Up, and a toast to you for making this the happiest birthday of all. I never expected such love from you. How can I thank you?" Another had me insisting that this Laufer-organized event was "my all-time best birthday." Still another had me accepting a poster from Sharon Lee, editor of the Laufer publication *TB Spectacular*. The caption quoted me as responding, "Gosh, Laufer's editors are so wonderful." Gosh, that sure does sound like me talking, all right: *"Gosh, Laufer's editors are so wonderful."*

And the editors informed the presumably lovesick young readers nationwide: "David wants all YOU to know that he loves you very much and without your love he couldn't have known happiness." And: "David wishes he could give YOU a hug and a kiss to know how much he appreciates your thinking of him." That's it, Chuck, just keep feeding them, feeding them.

I was touched by the care fans took in sending me gifts, particularly the handmade ones, although I hardly had any use for them. But I suspect most fans had no concept of just how many other fans were sending me things—or realized that by the age of twenty-one, thanks largely to my concert work, I was already a millionaire. A fan who sent a really great birthday gift knew she might even be lucky enough to see her name in one of the magazines. They'd print a line saying, "David is going to use the hand-knitted afghan sent by fan Eileen Fry of Belmar, New Jersey, as his bedspread," and other fans would rush to send similar gifts that they knew I would keep close to me.

However, one person who really should have been cognizant of my age—but, unfortunately for me, did not—was the lawyer for Screen Gems (or its parent company, Columbia Pictures Industries) who drew up the contract signing me to them. You see, when I signed that remarkably exploitative contract with them, I was under twenty-one years of age. And since twenty-one was the legal age of adulthood at that time, the contract would only have been valid had they gotten either my father or my mother to sign it. But they just assumed I was an adult. They didn't check. And they neglected to ask for a parent's signature. That one little oversight would wind up costing Screen Gems a lot of money.

I mean, the show went into production with me being paid just $600 a week—little more than scale. They promised to give me modest raises in subsequent years. With that contract, they believed they had acquired all the rights to my name, voice, and likeness for seven years. At some point, however, someone from Screen Gems finally realized they'd made a mistake and that the contract was not legally valid. The work I'd been doing for Screen Gems and its affiliate, Bell Records, was not under contract at all.

Rather sheepishly, they asked if I could just get one of my parents to sign the contract so it would be binding. Ruth Aarons, of course, knew better than to do that. Now for the first time we clearly had the upper hand. She went in to see them on my behalf. By this point the show had been running for more than a year; my record sales were in the millions; I was on the covers of magazines. I was *the* hot young dude. Screen Gems and Bell Records needed me.

Ruth told them: "Look, you've mistreated this person badly. You're making millions of dollars off David Cassidy and are paying him just six hundred a week. I want you to remove his name, his voice, his likeness, from all the records and tapes and everything. I want you to simply take him out of everything you've been using him in unless you're willing to make him a profit participant." The first time she said it they freaked! These were of course thieves, dear friends.

Never before had anyone gone in and had any nuts with these people. I mean, they raped everybody who ever worked for them. The Monkees got nothing. Actors got nothing. The artists always got robbed. Who got the profits? The corporations. Screen Gems and Bell Records stood to make hundreds of millions of dollars off me; yet they were content to pay me less than they would have paid guys in middle management. Ruth said she wouldn't stand for it. She was about to break the precedent.

We renegotiated my contract. In the end, I wound up owning a piece of the *net* profits—which at that point was unprecedented. Columbia Pictures and Screen Gems had never given up a piece to anybody. My base salary shot up to $4,000 a week. And as a token of their appreciation, Screen Gems also gave me a new Corvette. (That's a classic move in Hollywood or the record industry, giving a performer a car. He's expected to feel grateful for the wonderful gift—and to be less inclined to check carefully whether he is being paid fairly.) I took the bait.

Under the contract I had originally signed, I was not to have been paid *anything* for making records. For that $600 a week, Screen Gems had acquired all rights to my name, voice, and likeness. But Ruth insisted I'd now have to be paid royalties for my records, too. We settled on the following terms: for all records issued under my own name (and the first David Cassidy single, "Cherish," was on the *Billboard* charts for twelve weeks, beginning November 6, 1971) and all Partridge Family recordings, I'd receive 5 percent of the net profits to $500,000, 6 percent to $1 million, 7 percent thereafter. This was a very good record deal in 1971. Today it would be three times that percent.

Ruth also insisted that I participate in the profits derived from all Partridge Family or David Cassidy merchandising—that is to say, anything that Screen Gems licensed using the Partridge Family or David Cassidy name, from a poster to a lunch box. Sounds good, right?

Ruth further insisted that the period the contract covered be shortened from seven years to four years. After four years, we figured we could probably negotiate an even better deal, or I could leave. We could get more money out of Screen Gems and Bell or go elsewhere and do better. Screen Gems took the attitude that they had made me a star, just like they had made the Monkees stars, and that I was raping them. They felt I was becoming too big for my boots. Screen Gems had helped launch my career—but now it was me that the public wanted. I had a notion that the *Partridge Family* TV show might even be holding me back. I didn't want to be tied down for seven long years. I wanted greater freedom to express myself as a creative artist. I wanted freedom to do whatever I chose after four years. And I wanted to be paid. I could envision my career continuing to grow in subsequent years—concerts, records, TV, and films. Screen Gems gave me most of the terms that I asked for.

I still wound up being paid a lot less money than I should have; Ruth was simply unsophisticated when it came to these areas. She didn't have experience in the record business or merchandising. She'd certainly never represented an idol before. Although we had no way of knowing it at the time we renegotiated the contract, Screen Gems actually wound up getting off very cheap.

One mistake we made in renegotiating was in agreeing to accept a percentage of net profits. We should have insisted upon a percentage of gross income. It was unheard-of, of course, at that time, but with clever accounting, a record company, for example, could claim that even if they grossed hundreds of millions of dollars on my records, their profits—and consequently the royalties they'd pay me—were actually surprisingly small. (At one point, we came to suspect that Bell Records was not paying me all that it should. We had an audit done, which indicated they owed me an additional $400,000. They then grudgingly gave me about half of that, which I accepted, knowing that if I fought them in a long court battle, I'd spend a fortune in attorneys' fees.) I wound up earning virtually nothing on merchandising—a total of $15,000—even though every time I turned around, someone was marketing another product bearing my name. They were making the money, not me. But Ruth and I were barely aware of what was going on in the merchandising field, and we simply let millions of dollars slip through our fingers. If we got a report that only six thousand David Cassidy posters had been sold in a certain period, at very little profit, we didn't challenge those figures. (By the time Ruth Aarons was managing my brother Shaun's career, in the late seventies, she watched marketing details much more carefully; I think Shaun made a million dollars off the sale of posters and related items, even though his career as a pop star didn't last as long as mine.)

I figured I was making so much money overall, particularly from my concerts—I could gross $35,000, $50,000, or more in one night—I didn't worry that I might be getting shortchanged here or there. How much could I spend, anyway? I was not a materialistic guy.

Everyone I knew respected Ruth Aarons for her wit and her knowledge. She'd come from an important theatrical family. I just naturally assumed that she—and the business manager she had with me, Lee Bush—knew all that was needed to know about the business. I was really impressed with her getting me a salary of

$4,000 a week for the TV show. You have to remember, I didn't have shit when I started out. In 1969 my total earnings for the *year* had been no more than $3,000. So I was delighted, in 1971, to be getting $4,000 a week. Salaries in show business, generally, weren't anywhere near as high then as they are today. The biggest star in television at that point—James Arness, who'd been doing *Gunsmoke* since 1955—was only making around $17,500 a week. The most Shirley Jones was ever paid for a motion picture was $250,000. Ruth assured me that between my TV show, records, and concerts, I could certainly count on making more than that figure each and every year.

Screen Gems had initially established a budget of about $120,000 per episode of *The Partridge Family*. If my salary had to be upped to $4,000, that was no problem for them; they could gladly accommodate it. *TV Guide* reported in 1972 that, due to the success of our TV show, records, and all of the assorted merchandising spin-offs, one Screen Gems bigwig was now referring to *"The Partridge Family* Money Machine." *The Partridge Family*, declared *TV Guide*, was "practically a branch of the U.S. Mint."

I guess I never heard those reports. I was too busy touring, filming, recording, and answering—for the umpteenth time—the same dumb questions from interviewers. Almost everyone wanted to know what I ate, what I drank, what I looked for in girls ("honesty" was my less-than-completely-honest reply), and how I liked working with my stepmother. One interviewer, who'd been around the block a lot more times than most of the others, had a more pertinent question to ask—even if I didn't grasp its significance at the time. Veteran *New York Post* columnist Earl Wilson didn't ask me any of the usual bullshit questions when we met in March of 1972. The big thing he wanted to know was, "Who's taking care of your money, David?" I told him, "Lee Bush, a business manager and accountant. I'm investing in oil . . . ."

CHAPTER 12

I could make my sex life *sound* much more rewarding than it often actually was for me. "Man, you should have seen all these naked chicks in my room." Guys talk to other guys like that. And I'd even talk to Susan Dey in pretty much the same way—she was the only woman back then that I really thought of as a close friend and confidant and not a sexual object. On Mondays I'd get to the studio where we filmed the TV show and I'd sometimes tell Susan about my escapades while on tour over the weekend. I'd tell her about how I'd had sex with some great-looking woman on the road or whatever. But even if the woman had actually been interesting, I knew I'd almost certainly never see her again. These were nearly all one-shot deals, and after a while I realized that emotionally they didn't add anything to my life. I yearned for some kind of a relationship. But with whom? Maybe I'd meet some chick on the set, and by our second date she'd be hinting how she'd love to be an extra on *The Partridge Family*. A lot of the women I met struck me as opportunists, using me or anyone to advance hoped-for acting careers, or were perhaps interested in me for my money. This ain't the real stuff. So I looked for something more.

Of all the actresses I dated, there was only one I really fell for or thought I had. Only one I really wanted to have a lasting relationship with. Meredith Baxter. She was a few years older than I was when she made a guest appearance on *The Partridge Family* and we began dating. If you can call it that. She'd just gotten divorced from her first husband and was living in a little house in Burbank with her two young children, trying to make it on her own as an actress. I really carried a serious torch for her. I never told anybody about it except Susan Dey, Shirley, and a couple of other friends. Meredith was a beautiful woman—warm, intelligent, independent, kind of a hippie at heart, like I was. She liked music, and would sit around and play guitar. She was also much more mature than I was. I may have been twenty-one, but emotionally I was still a teenager.

Everything Meredith and I did was secretive, because I didn't want to tip the tabloids. We usually simply went to Meredith's house or mine.

I was dating her in one of the worst periods of my life. I mean, nobody worked longer or harder than I did. The television show kept me tied up from six in the morning to seven at night, at which point I'd go straight to the recording studio—no dinner, except for a sandwich I'd eat there.

I had so little free time that days and weeks would often go by without my seeing Meredith at all. She, I'm sure, interpreted it like I wasn't too interested in her. But it honestly wasn't that; I was just a working machine in those days. Although I wasn't with her a whole lot, whenever I was with her the time was great. I thought I might be in love with her. I'm sure that to her it didn't seem like I loved her, because I wasn't around very much. That would sometimes grow frustrating for me, but I was on such a roll in the rest of my life I didn't know what to do. If I couldn't see her as much as I might have liked, I'd at least call her every couple of days and talk to her. I figured that eventually my life would grow less hectic, and then we could really get to spend some time together. Wrong again, paleface. Instead, my life grew more hectic.

After we had been dating for about a month, I got home from work one Friday night—I was supposed to go on the road early the next morning—and Ruth Aarons telephoned me. She was the only person at that time who had my direct phone number.

She said, "I want to pack up everything you've got; you're leaving your house."

I said, "What are you talking about?"

"In about fifteen minutes there's going to be someone buzzing at your gate, who's from the FBI. Go with him. This isn't a joke. There's a legitimate kidnapping threat." Perfect.

The Los Angeles Police Department had been tipped by a very reliable source. Two guys planned on kidnapping me, and hoped to collect a multimillion-dollar ransom from my family and Screen Gems–Columbia Pictures. In my mind I went to the worst scenarios: *They're going to kill me.* I moved out of my house. I lived in the Holiday Inn on Highland Avenue. Initially I had members of the FBI in the room on one side of mine, and the LAPD in the room on the other. For extra security, I hired a bodyguard, a Pinkerton man, who lived in my room.

We didn't want to tip anybody off. I simply had to bring this guy with me everywhere I went, as if he were some good old friend. Problem was I didn't know him. He never said much; he just stuck to me like glue. If I got up to go anywhere—even to the john— he'd walk along with me. He'd stand outside, casually keeping an eye out. He was a muscular fellow—the bodybuilder type—maybe thirty, thirty-two years old. And I was this rather slight, androgynous-looking, longhaired twenty-one-year-old (my stand-in on *The Partridge Family*, if you can believe it, was a girl); I looked about sixteen. Everyone at work was convinced we were lovers. "David's gone around the bend!"

I restricted my activities. To minimize my vulnerability, I went almost nowhere except to work. I took things one day at a time. The days turned into weeks. I was in agony.

The only public function I went to in that period was the annual Golden Apple Awards presentation. They'd told me beforehand that I had won a Golden Apple. The ceremony took place at the Beverly Hills Hotel, and all of Hollywood was there. The police and FBI were especially fearful that an attempt to kidnap me would be made there, where maintaining security was difficult. This would be the day they'd make the snatch.

At the hotel, there were waiters and doormen who were really members of the FBI and the LAPD. I dressed in a jeans jacket, jeans, and a T-shirt, everyone else was dressed up. I was so scared I was going to get kidnapped that when I got up to accept my award, I was shaking. I was looking at everyone in the room like, *Maybe these are the guys who are out to get me.*

In accepting my award I said just two words: "Thank you." That was it. And I'm usually a pretty voluble guy. But I just walked off. The audience must have thought, "That's it? Thank you? What a stiff!"

At one point during the awards I had to get up to go to the bathroom. There were twenty-seven people who got up simultaneously and followed me there. I didn't know who might be trying to protect me, who might be trying to get me, or who was just trying to take a leak.

I fantasized about the day when this mess would be over

with, and I could pick up with Meredith where we'd left off. I was so weighted down with my own problems, I really wasn't thinking what she might be going through . . . kid stuff, pure kid stuff.

I'd never lived in the real adult world. I'd gone straight from fooling around as a teenager, living with my parents, to the highly artificial world of TV stardom. In a lot of ways I didn't see the futility of my career. It was best characterized by having to live with this Pinkerton bodyguard instead of with someone who mattered to me, the way most people my age were able to do.

My life as a pop star was like being in a hurricane most of the time. As if someone had completely ripped up my sense of reality and said, *Here, try this on for a while, instead.* Nobody looked at me the same way people had before I'd become famous. No one could really get near me anymore. And the more people who related to me as this guy from merchandising, marketing, and the television show, the more lost the real person became. I'd started out trying to be a serious actor and become this supposed demigod, *living* in fear in a Holiday Inn, accompanied everywhere by this inexplicable tall, silent, muscular guy.

And what did I think would happen once this whole kidnapping episode was behind me? I guess I thought that I could resume touring, doing TV, and making records as both David Cassidy and the Partridge Family and somehow maintain a successful relationship with Meredith Baxter. Yeah, that'll happen . . .

It still didn't hit me—I really wasn't mature enough to see it—that the kidnapping threat wasn't the real problem. The way I was living my life as a constantly working television actor/recording artist/concert performer, it would be impossible for me to have a real relationship with anyone. There wasn't enough free time in my schedule to have a relationship with myself, let alone another human being. But I just couldn't grasp that. I was totally lost.

Finally, after about a month had passed since I'd first been told there was a pending kidnap threat, we assumed the would-be kidnappers had given up. I had seen no signs of danger. Maybe it had been a false alarm all along, or maybe they'd been scared off. The FBI and police concluded things were all right before I finally did. Then I let the Pinkerton guard go and tried to get things started up again with Meredith. I don't think so, pal.

Her life had moved ahead without me. While I'd been worried about possible kidnappers, she'd fallen in love with someone else. The producers of *The Partridge Family* had hired Meredith and David Birney to costar in a new series called *Bridget Loves Bernie*, and I learned she'd started having a relationship with her costar. Meredith and I spent one final weekend together after they became involved, which I'm sure David Birney never knew about. Then Meredith broke off the relationship with me for good.

I tried to tell her of my sorrow. She just said, "I can't see it. You're doing all of these different things and I never see you." It was hard for me to accept that. Even though there were millions of people who loved me and worshipped me and wanted me, I needed something else.

Meredith and David did their TV series at the same studio where I did mine, right next to me. I'd see them every day together. It broke my heart. Eventually, of course, they got married (and some years later, divorced), and eventually, too, I got over her. I continued to fantasize about having a real relationship with a real person, about having a date out in public without having people going stupid over you. Maybe I hadn't been college material, but I envied my old high school classmates who'd gone on to college. And I envied those others who'd gone on to "normal" jobs. Either of those paths seemed preferable to the one I'd taken. I started longing to have any other career but my own. It may sound absurd now but it's true: there I was—rich and famous, a star on TV, on records, and in concerts—wishing at times I could have been just some thoroughly ordinary, anonymous guy instead. I'd fantasize about what it would be like to work a real man's job. Like, say, a soda jerk or a bartender.

CHAPTER
13

Whenever I stepped out onto the concert stage, I liked to think I was there simply to entertain people. I was serious about my show. I wanted to be the best entertainer I could.

TV Guide, for one, perceived my role in the business differently. They said that in my public appearances, I served in effect as a shill—not just for the *Partridge Family* TV show but for a seemingly endless supply of products bearing its name or mine. I hate to admit that's true—certainly it had never been my intention to become anything like that—but in a way it was.

The industry found me highly marketable and exploited my appeal to the maximum. My face was used to sell pictures, posters, magazines, and even special stamps for fan mail. It wound up on cereal boxes—General Foods paid a great deal to Screen Gems for that right. I had no say in how my name, voice, or likeness was used, what products I appeared to be endorsing. That was all handled by Screen Gems. They wanted to get everything they could out of the craze for David Cassidy and the Partridge Family.

There were Partridge Family coloring books, comic books, David Cassidy music books, and just plain books. By mid-1972 Popular Library had published a dozen Partridge Family paperback novels, the best-selling of which had reportedly sold a million copies. I never saw a dime. Popular Library paid 5 percent of the cover price to Screen Gems. There were Partridge Family paper dolls, regular dolls, diaries, and astrological charts. Schoolchildren could carry David Cassidy lunch boxes. Their older sisters could spend their summers lying atop beach towels bearing full-length portraits of me; those were a popular premium offered by Hi-C fruit beverages. There was even a plastic David Cassidy guitar. I wish I owned one now.

Screen Gems tried to tell my manager that licensing items really wasn't a very lucrative business, but reports in the press suggested otherwise. For example, the *New York Times* reported that in the months of April and May 1971, Screen Gems' royalties from Partridge Family bubble gum alone were $59,000. I was supposed to get 15 percent of that. But I never did. They never accounted to me. That, dear friends, is stealing.

With great fanfare, Kate Greenaway Industries, a reputable, established children's clothing manufacturer, introduced a Partridge Family collection (for which, the press reported, they agreed to pay Screen Gems a licensing fee of $10,000 a month for fifteen months), to be marketed with the message "David Cassidy will love you in these Kate Greenaways." Greenaway advertising director Alan Jackson noted, "The Partridge Family is what's happening in America today." Greenaway vice-president Neil Goldberger observed, "David Cassidy is the love object of thousands of ten-to-thirteen-year-old girls. We hope these young ladies will be equally as excited by our Partridge Family collection as they are by him. After all, if you get a girl at six, she's a customer till ten or eleven." And so on and so on.

Companies marketed a Partridge Family Game for the whole family, a David Cassidy guitar for boys, and a Susan Dey sewing kit for girls. Buyers of the latter were encouraged to "make an outfit for David Cassidy." With seemingly any product, they could find some way to trade on my name. I took a little vacation in Hawaii, where I strung some shells together on a string. I was photographed wearing that homemade necklace. The next thing I knew, magazines were talking about how much I loved to wear those pooka shells, and ads began appearing telling kids that if they'd just mail in their money, they too could soon be the proud owners of a necklace like mine. At my concerts I'd see thousands of kids who had proudly bought these necklaces in emulation of me, even though, by that time, I was no longer wearing anything like that myself. I thought it was hysterical at first, all of these kids copying me. Then I thought it was disgusting, the way kids were being conned into buying things they didn't need because those things were supposedly connected with me. (And I again, of course, never made jack off those pooka shell necklaces; others did.) I looked around and thought, what have I done?

What really pissed me off is that I had no control over the quality of the merchandise. They could make anything that had my name on it—a cheap perfume, an unimaginative toy, a corny David Cassidy "wiggle postcard," even a David Cassidy pillowcase (so girls could, in effect, sleep with me)—and sell it. That was really disturbing. There were massive sales of this stuff, grossing untold millions of dollars, and I received virtually no payment. Columbia Pictures and Screen Gems made who knows how much money. I got a token sum. Once. Fifteen thousand dollars total. Are you ready? Yep, that's your share.

My manager tried to get statements from them, but the statements always reflected nothing, as if no one was making any profit on these things. We were very unsophisticated about merchandising and had no idea how many units any items were selling. You must remember, there wasn't anyone to learn from yet; no precedent. But the Partridge Family and David Cassidy merchandise was being sold worldwide. It was all over Europe, England, Germany, Belgium, Hong Kong, Japan, Australia—everywhere.

The *Partridge Family* TV show started in the U.S., Canada, and Hong Kong in the fall of 1970. By early 1971 we were also being seen in Mexico, Central America, the Caribbean, Brazil, Thailand, and Japan. By the end of 1971 we'd added England, Ireland, Spain, Portugal, Peru, Chile, Colombia, Zambia, the Philippines, Australia, and New Zealand. By early 1972 *The Partridge Family* was in Greece and some of the Arab world.

Screen Gems said yes to anyone who wanted to license the use of my name or the Partridge Family name for a product. The gag around Hollywood was that the only opportunity for exploitation that Screen Gems had missed was auctioning off my gallbladder. And that joke wasn't far from the mark, since there actually *were* fans who wrote asking if they could have my gallbladder—or at the very least, one of the gallstones I'd passed. A lock of my hair was a more common written request from fans. One company's proposal to market genuine locks of my hair sealed inside plastic was, I'm happy to say, turned down, I later found out.

The letters I read from young fans often had a plaintive innocence. One girl explained her interest in me this way: "I thought you sounded like a nice person. And I really don't meet up with nice people." Another young one confessed: "I always dreamed I was going steady with you, but now I blush whenever I think about it. I heard you are twenty years old." Fans vowed their eternal love for me, revealed that they'd written their names and mine all over their notebook covers, and had plastered their school lockers with photos and clippings about me. One fan wrote: "I hope my letters have been getting to you. I'm just wondering because I haven't gotten any back from you. If you think I have a boyfriend, I don't . . ." Twenty to thirty thousand times a week.

So many of these fans seemed to actually expect me to personally write back to them. Instead they'd receive invitations from the Laufer Company to read *Partridge Magazine* (by mid-1972 they were peddling 400,000 copies a month at fifty cents per), join the official David Cassidy Fan Club (by mid-1972 they had 200,000 members, paying two dollars per year), and purchase assorted photos and posters at prices to fit any budget. The company would encourage fans to send an extra fifty cents if they wanted "rush handling," and countless girls in the thralls of puppy love—imagining they'd be making contact with me that much quicker—would gladly cough up the extra four bits. That line made me laugh: "Please enclose an additional fifty cents for rush handling." I think they would have been more honest if they'd simply printed: "Please enclose an additional fifty cents for Chuck Laufer." All of those extra fifty centses sure added up.

Laufer was an interesting character. I didn't care for him myself because I always knew he just viewed me as someone to make money off of, but I have to admit he knew the teen-idol business better than just about anyone. He had quit his job as an English teacher to launch one of the very first teen fan magazines created, back in 1954, and had soon followed it up with others, realizing he could just as easily run photos and stories about a pop star simultaneously in four different publications as in one. His timing was perfect. In the mid-fifties rock and roll was just coming in. And an affluent teen market was emerging in this country. Kids were spending money freely on records, movies, clothes, and more. They wanted their own heroes, to give them a sense of identity as a generation, and he tapped into their desires effectively. By the time I came onto the scene, he had the business of exploiting teen heroes down to a science. He told me he figured we were each good for about a two-year run before the magazines would have to start hyping someone new.

He explained to reporters his theory of the two-year cycle. "There *has* to be a teenage idol, but the girls outgrow them. When they're eleven to fourteen, they can have a nice, safe love affair with somebody like Davy Jones, Bobby Sherman, or David Cassidy. By the time they're sixteen, they're having dates, and they don't need them anymore." And after a couple of years, he felt, the artist would likely be suffering from overexposure. People would simply be eager to look at a new face.

I hated to think that the roots of my popularity might be as Laufer seemed to believe. My career still seemed to be building in intensity. In 1972 my TV show was in the top twenty, my concert grosses were huge and growing, I felt like I was *the* guy—yet when I'd talk to Laufer he seemed to be all but anticipating that soon my career would begin to slow down. He'd been running me on his magazine covers every issue since mid-1970. Public interest in me, he admitted, was feverish, but he felt that fevers had a way of suddenly breaking.

Although there were no signs yet of my popularity cresting, Laufer said he was already looking around to see who might replace me as the next teen hero. And once I'd been replaced, he believed, I'd be history; he'd seen the pattern played out so many times before. He reminded me how hot Bobby Sherman had been for two years—records, concerts, posters. Sherman had been practically created by television. His frequent appearances on *Shindig* had led to a featured role on TV's *Here Come the Brides* (1968–70). But when that series had gone off the air, his concert bookings and record sales dramatically fell off. The producers of *The Partridge Family* tried to revive interest in Sherman by having him guest-star on our show; they used our show to spin off a new series for him, but it quickly died; he was viewed in the industry as a has-been. I thought he was sad.

Laufer reminded me that he had run Bobby Sherman's picture on some thirty consecutive magazine covers before running the first small photo of me. Then the photos of me got bigger and Sherman's got smaller, until Sherman's stopped appearing in the magazines altogether; public interest in him had burned itself out. It was disconcerting for me to hear that kind of talk. I didn't want to believe it could be true—or relevant to my career. After all, I told myself, my popularity was much bigger than Sherman's had been. My career was going to last. I mean, Sidney Skolsky, one of the oldest and most respected of the syndicated Hollywood columnists, had declared flatly (February 5, 1972): "David Cassidy is to today's youngsters what Elvis was to his generation's youngsters." I believed that to be so.

To any reporter who was astute enough to suggest that Laufer was probably making a lot of money out of promoting me in his magazines, he moaned that he was also spending a lot of money. In mid-1972 he figured he was paying thirty people to work on me— whether writing about me, photographing me, opening my fan mail, or processing mail-order requests. He had considerable overhead and had to give Screen Gems a cut off the top of everything he made off me.

Laufer's biggest competitor (Laufer used to say to me things like, "If *only* we could merge, we could *control* the teen market") was the late Gloria Stavers. Her top publication (with a circulation in 1972 of 1.2 million) was the rather classy *16*. She, too, did a record-setting business in peddling David Cassidy–related products (for which she paid Screen Gems a 5 percent licensing fee), hyped via house ads. She had made money off other teen heroes before, but never like she was making off of me. As she told one reporter in 1972, the David Cassidy Love Kit, available exclusively to her readers, was "the super-biggest thing we've ever had. I ought to know. I created it." Costing two dollars, the David Cassidy Love Kit included one life-sized full-length portrait of me, one autographed poster of me *three times* life size, one photo album covering my entire childhood (I loaned to various magazines priceless original childhood photos, most of which I never saw again), the supposed story of my life (considerably cleaned up), no fewer than forty wallet-sized photos of me, a special "love message from David," and—Stavers' master coup for the truly ardent David Cassidy fan—a "lovers' card with his name and yours."

When the *New York Times* asked me why I thought I had become a teen idol, I answered carefully: "Who can say why one person is singled out? Maybe because of the way I talk or look. Possibly because I'm uncomplicated, clean. There's no threat involved." Man, that sounded deep, didn't it?

Even I was amazed at how big interest in *The Partridge Family* and me grew. The thing spun into a megadeal—nominated for Grammy and Golden Globe awards, none of which we won. Our show and music weren't quite creditable enough; they were too commercial, too kid-oriented. That I got nominated for Grammys seemed pretty extraordinary to me, considering that before I was hired for *The Partridge Family* I had never even had aspirations of becoming a recording artist.

Partridge Family singles, given great exposure by our show, sold millions, too. "I Woke Up in Love This Morning" made *Billboard*'s "Top Pop Singles" chart for eleven weeks, beginning August 14, 1971; "It's One of Those Nights (Yes Love)" for eight weeks, beginning December 18, 1971.

My debut album under my own name, *Cherish*, went gold. It made the charts for twenty-three weeks (peaking at number 15), beginning February 12, 1972. My second album, *Rock Me Baby*, charted for seventeen weeks (peaking at number 41). After "Cherish," which sold nearly 2 million singles, I had three more singles under my own name on the charts in 1972: "Could It Be Forever," "How Can I Be Sure," and "Rock Me Baby."

And I was giving sold-out concerts in the biggest halls, arenas, and stadiums in the world—even the Houston Astrodome. The level of success just blew me away. I was swept up in it. To become that famous all over the world—everywhere—it was pretty phenomenal. To capture the imagination of a whole generation of people is a difficult thing to do. Very few people have had the kind of impact upon a whole generation as I felt I was having.

I knew there were some people who hated me as a performer, who viewed me with utter contempt. As some pretty-face, no-talent sellout. They were entitled to their feelings. People seemed to either love me or hate me. Fortunately for me, the percentage that did love me loved me a lot. There's an old saying in the business that if you get one percent of the population to really love you, you're the biggest star in the world. And when you think about it, yeah, they're right.

CHAPTER
14

Remember the diving horse trick? In 1972 I broke the attendance record at the famed Steel Pier in Atlantic City, doing three shows in one very long day.

When I arrived in Atlantic City, there were 50,000 kids absolutely jamming this pier, waiting for me. There was only one way on and one way off the Steel Pier. To get to the performance hall, I'd have to somehow get through the solid mass of fans. And security was almost nonexistent—they had two guys at the artists' entrance at the stage . . . it was a joke.

For the first show, around midday, I arrived and left via an ambulance. That sort of worked. The crowd parted enough so that the ambulance, with lights flashing and siren blaring, could get through. But some fans guessed I was inside. My cover was blown, and between the ambulance and the hall, I got grabbed a few times. We knew we couldn't use the ambulance again.

For the second show we needed to be more creative. I walked the entire length of the Steel Pier—right through the whole crowd waiting to see David Cassidy—disguised as a woman. I put on my usual hip-hugger jeans, but instead of my sneakers I slipped into a pair of clogs. I put on a woman's wig, glasses, lipstick, rouge— the whole deal. It scared the shit out of me when I glanced in a mirror, because I really looked like a female. As I checked myself out in drag, I thought, *Well, shit! I actually look pretty good.* It worked like a charm, but I hated disguising myself as a woman.

By the third show, in the evening, I just pushed my hair up in my hat. I pulled the hat all the way down over my face, put on a pair of shades, and raised the collar of my windbreaker up as high as possible. I walked with one of my publicists, a girl name Bryna, as if we were in love. I put my arm around her. I looked right at her as I walked. I think we even kissed a little. Nobody paid attention to us as we worked our way through the crowd. My heart was pounding because the fans were packed all around me. I was actually touching them, rubbing shoulders with them. Finally, when I was just a few steps before the stage door, somebody spotted me and grabbed my hat. My hair came tumbling down and every- body could see it was me. Instant insanity! Chaos. Screaming. I managed to make it inside the building, slam the door shut, and yell for security. If it had happened ten feet earlier, I would have been dead. The fans were on poor Bryna, who hadn't made it inside the building. Fifty million screams of adolescent sexual seething!

I always tried to get out of a concert hall before fans realized I'd left. I'd do my last number, fly off the stage, and make it to a waiting car while the band was still playing and the audience was still roaring, hoping for another encore. Sometimes I'd dive into the back of the car and find a woman waiting for me. I remember in Bangor, Maine, a promoter surprised me by having two women ("a special little treat for you, David") in the car, wearing nothing but little string bikinis. It was thirty below out. "We're your love slaves," and in seconds they whipped out the oil. That sort of surprise could put a smile on any young buck's face.

Success is infectious. So naturally I got used to breaking records in my concert appearances. I filled some of the biggest stadiums in the world. I broke the Rolling Stones' record for number of consecutive shows at Wembley Stadium. I did six or eight sold-out shows there. The Stones had only been able to do five.

On my second trip to England, about a year after the first, the hysteria of the fans was even greater than the first time. No hotel in London would take me. So my manager rented Liz Taylor's yacht. You know what my fans did? They jumped into the Thames. You know what the Thames is like? Filthy, freezing, and contaminated. This was pan-fucking-demonium. Every dock, there'd be cars, boats. They had to have the police pick me up on a police boat, then take me to a dock where they'd have a car waiting for me with security. Just so they could get me on the television shows, to do a promotion.

I had no idea what England was actually like until I went back quietly by myself in 1984, when all of that early-seventies public hysteria over me was just a faint, long-lost memory. I had never been through Heathrow Airport as an ordinary person until 1984, though I'd been there six times.

On the second trip the press wasn't quite as kind to me. The first time I went to England, everyone in the press was great. They loved me. I was unknown and new. They treated me like a hero. The color supplement to the English *Evening Standard* put my face on the cover with a headline reading simply, "Welcome David Cassidy." That was typical.

The second time, I noticed little digs in the press. They tried to find little things about me to criticize. Find a nerve. I think they began to feel resentful of the fact that I was an American doing so well in England, and maybe taking away some attention worldwide from British pop attractions who'd dominated the music business for years.

One thing that was frustrating to me was that writers rarely seemed to write thoughtful critiques of my shows, or even bothered reviewing me or the material at all. They were more interested in covering the spectacle: the money I was making, the fans I was drawing, the number of people who fainted or were injured at my concerts—almost anything other than how well or poorly I performed. The reporters were always amazed at the seemingly boundless enthusiasm of my fans. British journalist Gordon Burn caught that enthusiasm well when he interviewed an unnamed London girl who, since she had first seen my picture two years earlier in a teen fan magazine called *Fabulous*, had amassed a collection of more than three hundred different photos of me (not including her posters), four scrapbooks, and a suitcase packed with magazines covering me. She explained I was her very favorite performer: "I saw him and all of a sudden something came over me. I know he always runs from his fans and hides and all that, but it doesn't put me off him. I don't think I'll ever go off of him. I just like him so much. I can't stop thinking about him. He's like any other boy but I suppose it's, like, he's a star and they're not. Most boys you meet are just ordinary, they're nothing. Course my boyfriend says he's a fairy but, well, no boys like him, do they?" She never actually got around to commenting on my abilities as a performer. Almost like, who cares if you're good or not, right?

Some British and American writers began to put me down because my appeal was so particularly strong with younger fans. I grew defensive. If my records were aimed primarily at thirteen-to-sixteen-year-olds, so what? Why is it adults believe their taste is any more weighty or meaningful? I still don't buy that one!

When critics belittled me, saying my appeal was just to kids,

I felt they were putting down my fans, not just me. And most of us, if we admit it, are still kids, and are just playing adults. I know I am. For me it's my essence. I empathized with my young fans.

What I tried to get across was that our teen years are no less significant than other periods of our lives. I think teenagers are often treated as second-class citizens. Adults say dismissively, "Oh, you know it's just puppy love—that doesn't mean anything." But when you're thirteen, it's the most important thing in your life. Like when you're thirty and you've just lost your job, or your marriage has broken up—isn't that the most important thing in your life?

I came to understand, too, that even the lightweight pop songs I recorded could have an enormous value to my fans. Songs like "I Think I Love You," "I Woke Up in Love This Morning," and "Cherish" may have been dismissed by some adults as simplistic, but I know that millions of teens, whose sexuality was just awakening, found those songs really articulated their feelings. I gave voice to emotions associated with adolescent relationships.

Intuitively I knew that what I was doing was more important than my most cynical critics realized. Sure, I could find flaws in the music myself. I felt wrenching conflicts about having made it as a music star without having picked, much less written, most of the songs I recorded. This pang grew. But I was aware I was bringing light into a lot of people's lives. And while I didn't always feel worthy of all the adulation I received, didn't always feel I was the best person they could have picked to worship as a hero, I also knew I was far from the worst. Better they were placing me on a pedestal than some hostile, antisocial asshole. Privately I may have groused I was more complex than the image that the public had bought into. But if kids had to have a hero, it's a good sign that they responded to one perceived as positive and honest.

I got sick of the endless photo shoots. And of seeing my face everywhere. On the posters being hawked outside of every concert

I played. (Most of those posters were unauthorized and I received no money from their sales. Anybody could take a photo of me—even from the pages of a fan magazine—and use it to make posters.) One newspaper writer said he could imagine my high school guidance counselor taking one look at my face and saying, "I'd advise you to go into the teen-idol business." I grew weary of photographers requesting things like, "And now, David, can you give us your pouty look?" And I'd do my finger-down-my-throat routine. But I didn't know how to simply say no. So my body began saying no for me. The skin infections on my face grew increasingly worse. We tried heavier makeups, which didn't always work. Some days my rather tactless road manager would actually tell the press, "David can't see anyone today. No photos! His acne is really bad." And the British press would make little cracks about my "spots," meaning pimples. They belittled me for having a young teen's problems with his skin—as if to say, he not only signs for teenyboppers, he's hardly much more than one himself. Ha! Pimples.

Playing Madison Square Garden—the biggest indoor venue in New York, America's biggest city—may have been my most prestigious public appearance to date, but one thing that made it especially important for me was that among the 20,000 people in attendance was my eighty-three-year-old grandfather, Fred Ward, proud to see how popular I was. And my mom, I knew how proud she was of me. It blew them all away.

That Madison Square Garden concert was a huge event. Bell Records put up a billboard in Hollywood announcing to the world at large (and the entertainment industry in particular) that I would be playing the Garden, three thousand miles away—and then almost immediately plastered onto the billboard the new message: "Sold out!"

The concert occurred March 11, 1972, and received extensive media coverage. *Life* magazine's managing editor, Ralph Graves, noted that before I appeared there was a one-hour warm-up period featuring other singers. (Those singers, whom he didn't seem to feel were worth mentioning by name, were Kim Carnes and Dave Ellingson.) He added that having a warm-up for me "was about as necessary as warming up an arena full of starving tigresses before throwing them a single Christian." Graves said he'd never heard anything like the virtually all-young-female audience's frenzied response to my performance: "You have to imagine the roar of a crowd at the moment Frazier knocked down Ali, while at the same moment Bobby Thomson was hitting his famous home run that put the Giants in the World Series, while simultaneously George Blanda was kicking a game-running field goal in the last five seconds, just as Ben Hur was on the last lap of his chariot race. Now put all that sound together on tape and play it without respite for an hour, not forgetting to raise the pitch up to a high C. The young girls in America have absolutely perfected the high-C shriek. My middle-aged eardrums were in shock after the first five minutes." Graves added that his twelve-year-old daughter told him, "I'll remember this day all the rest of my life." It made me smile, that one.

The showbiz bible, *Variety*, got to what it considered the most significant thing about the event in the first paragraph: from that one concert I had grossed a whopping $130,000. For 1972 that was a huge take. As to my performance, *Variety*'s judgment was that "Cassidy's well-choreographed act consisted mainly of waving his rear (in tight, white pants) to his adoring public." They said I fronted to the orchestra for one instrumental number at my "wiggling best." But they admitted the squealing teen and preteen girls seemed thrilled by every moment, even my mumbled introductions to songs, like when I told the audience that "I Think I Love You" described "how I feel about you."

Lillian Roxon of the *Daily News* noted that at the Garden I was "wiggling like Monroe in *Niagara*," although she felt I "was not one half as comfortable with it as, say, Michael Jackson. . . ."

The *New York Post*'s pop music writer, Alfred G. Aronowitz, fumed about my performance: "There is something obscene about selling sex to pre-pubescent little girls as if it was apple pie. . . . The way David swung his torso around, there was no question that he knew what those girls wanted to see."

The *New York Times* assigned both a features writer, Angela Taylor, and a music critic, Don Heckman, to cover my concert. Taylor reported that Madison Square Garden security guards had never seen anything like my frenzied fans. She noted it was startling to hear a second grader yelling, "I don't care if he's old. He's beautiful. Give him to me!"

Music critic Heckman declared the event was "less a concert than a symbolic announcement of what pop music might become." He described me as "the current idol of almost every 13-year-old girl in America," and "Cassidy is a still-developing singer with a pleasantly bland voice and a notable absence of rhythmic vitality. . . . But the significant element here is sensuality and theater, not music." He said I left 20,000 fans thoroughly satisfied, but added he suspected that their devotion to me "had more to say about the manipulative powers of television and recording than it did about David Cassidy." Maybe so. But here's my take . . .

I remember my people were thrilled by all of the publicity the concert generated, not to mention the huge box-office gross. Of course we had some unexpected expenses to contend with. My frenzied fans managed to destroy six limousines.

When the concert was finished, I ran off the stage, and two burly security men wrapped me in an army blanket and threw me in the trunk of a Toyota. They sent limousines out, which fans followed, while the Toyota headed off, unnoticed, in another direction. By the time the fans realized they'd been tricked, it was too late; I was gone.

About four blocks later, we stopped; I hopped out of the trunk and got into the backseat of this Toyota. All the hotels in Manhattan were swarming with fans looking for me. None of the good hotels in Manhattan would take me anymore. My musicians could—and did—stay at such places, but not me.

I was driven instead to some dump out in Queens, a cheap motel, where a room had been reserved for me under an alias. Fifteen minutes after starring in the most publicized concert in the world, I was dropped off—still wearing my white stage jumpsuit, which was drenched in sweat—at a shabby Queens motel. I didn't know where I was. I had no money and no clothes except for what I was wearing. I stayed in the bathtub for an hour and a half, alone. I waited for someone to call or come and get me. I had nothing. I didn't know where anybody was. I understood why Marilyn Monroe couldn't get a date on Saturday night. I lay there, scratched my head, and thought, *What am I doing this for?*

CHAPTER 15

Remember my father's pursuit of fame? Well, as I became more and more famous, we saw less of each other. Things had never been great between us, and my success only seemed to add to the tension. I think it happened for me so quickly it infuriated him. I now believe he was jealous.

For years he was upstaged by his wife. And then beginning in 1970, he was upstaged by me. He became known as Shirley Jones' husband and David Cassidy's father. It drove him around the bend. In his heart, I'm sure, he *was* proud of me; he genuinely *did* care about me. But he was frustrated. His ego was bent out of shape.

And by the early seventies he was drinking like a fish every night. Although he denied he had an alcohol problem, he obviously did. He lived his life in a constant state of denial. There were times when I overdid it. But my drinking hadn't become a problem for me, like it was for my dad. And he had a mean streak in him that surfaced when he drank.

I understood my father's frustrations; he'd worked forty years in the business and now I was the one getting on the cover of *Life* magazine; my appeal was being analyzed in the august pages of *The New Yorker*. He'd never achieved that kind of success. But just because his feelings were hurt, I wasn't going to kowtow to him like a child the way my brothers did.

That's why I was glad I never really lived with him. Whenever I was with him for a few weeks, while growing up, I found him an impossibly strict disciplinarian. So overbearing. I vowed I'd never be like him when I became a parent. And I've tried hard to keep that vow. Shaun has turned out to be a very good parent as well; perhaps we're both overcompensating because of what we suffered as kids.

He had such selfish household rules. He'd have silent periods when he didn't want to be disturbed. In the morning you couldn't make any noise and wake him up. Four boys, right? When he wasn't working, he and his friends would likely stay up until 3 A.M. The next morning, if he was awake by 10:30, that was early; noon was more likely. You try and tell kids they've got to be quiet till noon because Daddy needs his rest.

The funny thing is, he could never see that he had any problems. By the early 1970s he was convinced *I* was the one with the problems. He'd complain to reporters that he didn't have access to me; that I'd gotten too big for my britches and was surrounding myself with hangers-on who barely knew who he was, that he couldn't get to see as much of me as he wanted to. (Yeah, right! Like he'd ever wanted to see a lot of me.) He couldn't conceal his resentment of my success. New York *Daily News* gossip columnist Robin Adams Sloan reported (July 13, 1972) that Jack Cassidy was "basking in reflected, teeth-gritting envy" of me, adding: "They say if you want to make friends with Jack nowadays, don't say anything to him about another show business star, little David." Yup, that's my dad.

One reporter tried to get me to say whether I thought my father or I was the star of the family. I responded curtly that I didn't consider myself part of my father's family; that his family consisted only of himself, Shirley, Shaun, Ryan, and Pat.

I wasn't the only one having difficulty getting along with him. Before the year was out, newspapers were reporting that Shirley Jones and Jack Cassidy had agreed to a trial separation. Their marriage sputtered along, off and on, for a few more years before finally collapsing. He was slowly destroying everything around him. The years of alcohol combined with the madness, and his life began to unravel.

Shirley explains: "It was clear to me that David himself was really suffering when he was going through the teen-idol syndrome, the screaming kids and the whole thing. Being the sensitive—and basically private—person that David is, it really got to him. The type of success David achieved had proved to be very difficult—not just for him, but for everyone who was around him. Jack was bothered by the fact that David hadn't worked long enough for everything he'd gotten. And he knew that kind of success often didn't last. David's mother also had difficulties as a result of his fame. One of the terrible problems his mother had was that everybody seemed to believe *I* was David's mother. Most people believed it then; most people still believe it today. His mother was not very happy about that, nor could I blame her. And having to go see him under an assumed name and all that crap that was necessary in order to avoid the fans and the press, and the hordes of police and security men around him—that was also terrible. David became a prisoner of his success. I wouldn't want anybody to go through that. Just think of what David went through. You make a lot of money, you have a lot of success, but it's all so fleeting. That's hard on a young person. Especially when, unexpectedly, one day you find it's all gone. . . . David's success was rough on the whole family. It was rough on his brothers, having to be the brothers of the great teen idol."

I asked Shaun how he experienced my success, and how he thought I might have changed as a result of it. "When it all began to happen for David, I was only eleven, so I was too young to have a great deal of insight as to who David was as a person. I mean, I didn't even know David sang until he did *The Partridge Family*. Up until then, my perception of David was simply as my half brother who I hung out with. And I loved hanging out with him. I thought he was a good older brother to me when we were around. He teased me a lot like I'd tease my younger brothers. But I loved going places in the car with him.

"Then suddenly he was acting on this TV show. And don't forget, *The Partridge Family* was not just any TV show. It was very popular and it was considered very 'wholesome.' So there I was, this kid whose mom and brother were starring in this wholesome show. And David's music was invariably described as 'wholesome,' too. So I acquired a 'Partridge Family' kind of image by association. And believe me, when you're a kid going into your teens—as I was when David's fame was reaching its peak—'wholesome' is not a cool thing to be. So I pushed hard to go the other direction, to establish a different identity with my peers. And I made it clear my musical tastes were 180 degrees different from *The Partridge Family*. My cultural icons were Led Zeppelin and the Stones. When I was thirteen, I had dreams of someday going into music—but the Partridge Family sound was the last thing I would have wanted to emulate.

"From my point of view, the most important changes I noticed in David as he became successful was that he just wasn't as accessible.

Time-wise, he just wasn't available as often as he had been before. I didn't feel really close to him. He became much more insulated.

"Looking back with the wisdom of an adult, I'd say that when success happens to anyone as early as it did for David—or, a few years later, for me—it can be damaging, because you end up being surrounded by a lot of sycophants. And that was certainly the case with David. (The same thing happened to me, too.) Had I been older, more experienced, I could have said to David something like, 'Don't wrap yourself up in Graceland, here.' He definitely had a bit of that going on."

I wasn't trying to deliberately isolate myself from my family or anyone else. Running an international career involving television, records, and concerts was exhausting. The only reason I was making millions of dollars was that I was working hard, doing as many shows as I could. During a two-year period of time, I was the highest-paid solo male artist in the world. I was playing huge venues. I could work one night and take in $70,000 or more. I talked to Ruth, my manager, three, four, five, or more times in a day. She was the only person I talked to so frequently; no one else had access like that. I was connected to her more tightly than to my parents. We had a business together, Daru Enterprises, Inc. ("Daru" came from the first two letters of my first name and hers.) My career was so unlike any others Ruth had handled before—she'd never had an artist with her anywhere near my commercial success— and she was learning a lot as she went along. The record business— this was all new to her. But I was doing so well, I had no cause to be concerned. And also, I was making an awful lot of money for Ruth. She had to hire several other people just to work on my career. Directly or indirectly, I was supporting a lot of folks.

But I trusted Ruth's judgment a thousand percent. There are mixed opinions about her. I thought she was great—a unique, in many ways bizarre, human being who lived and breathed show business. She always championed me and was a close ally of mine. A number of people, including members of my family, don't agree with my assessment of her, and in fact actually came to hate her. My mother, for instance. Even Shirley eventually decided to leave Ruth. But I loved Ruth and would have done anything for her. I thought she was right on top of things. And she was until the last months of her life. Talking to her wasn't the hassle talking to my parents could be. I didn't have the energy for a lot of idle chitchat anyway.

No matter how successful you are, you have to sometimes wonder how long it will last. I did all the time. It was gratifying reading articles saying I was causing more excitement in the pop music field than anyone had in five years, that no one since the Beatles had drawn so many screaming fans to airports. But every front-runner has to worry who might be gaining on him. I'd be filled with self-confidence one moment, touched by pangs of self-doubt the next. If a concert didn't go over quite as well as expected, I'd wonder if it was just a meaningless blip on the graph or possibly a first sign of trouble. When I returned to the Wildwood, New Jersey, Convention Hall in the summer of 1972, *Variety* noted with approval that I'd become "a well rehearsed and disciplined talent." But they also noted: "Although the Wildwood area was jammed with over 400,000 tourists, Cassidy did not repeat last season's bonanza business when he had even the aisles crowded in the 3,800 seat hall. This time, he pulled only slightly over 2,000 to each of two shows on Sunday." *Variety* thought the problem was due to some poor press. But was that it? Were the concerts not promoted as well as they should have been? Or were the fans who'd been dying to see me last summer simply not so eager to see me a second or third time? Reporters always asked me, "How long do you think your popularity can last?"

My concerts were selling out, and my fees for appearances were still rising. But mass opinion can change unpredictably. Why? Who knows? In 1972 I was just as "in" as bell bottoms were. There were moments when I'd wonder how long it would be before bell bottoms were "out." Along with, perhaps, David Cassidy.

One seventeen-year-old fan from Long Island, Penny Bergman, told the *New York Times* she'd be hesitant about admitting to friends at school she was still a fervent David Cassidy fan. "He's known as a teenage idol. I'm too old."

Even one thirteen-year-old insisted, "Just about everybody in my class thinks he's gross. He's for those younger kids who read dopey fan magazines."

But a lot of kids, all across America, were buying those "dopey fan magazines," and avidly reading the articles relentlessly being ground out with headlines like, "You Know Your Love for David Cassidy Is Deep and True," "Why No Girl Can Make Him Happy," and (a classic), "Would You Like to Know When I Was Born, How Old I Am, My Coloring—and All My Measurements?"

The people around me assured me I was just as popular as ever. They pointed out that, in 1972, we were conquering the British pop record market in a way no American had in years. In May of 1972 a David Cassidy single with "Could It Be Forever" on one side and "Cherish" on the other reached number 2 on the British charts. My career as an international pop star was still growing.

I increasingly had contact only with the people I felt safe with, my inner circle: my head of security, Billy Francis; my personal photographer, Henry Diltz; and of course, Sam. I considered Elliot Mintz a close friend in the seventies, too, although it's hard to admit that now. I was impressed that he was close to people like John Lennon and Yoko Ono; he seemed to know everybody. He had a talk show on KPFK, a free radio station in Los Angeles. He was very much the voice of change and political thrust in the sixties and continued in that role into the seventies. Then he started doing documentary kind of shows, profiling rock celebrities. He came along on one of my European tours and did an audio documentary—just kept the tape rolling the whole time. Eventually I agreed to a lot of frank, in-depth, off-the-record interviews with him; he said he wanted background for a proposed biography of me, which he never wrote. He later attempted to sell those raw tapes to publishing companies without my authorization, for which I can never forgive him. I finally concluded he was just another parasite, eager to find any way to make money off knowing me. So life goes on.

I met so many parasites. For a while in 1972 I was seeing a girl named Lynn, who was into photography. I met her in New York at the Garden. Sweet little Lynnie—she had every move. She went from rock star to rock star. She sold to a magazine photos of me that she took when we were together. That was it. I blew her off at that point. I just said, "I really don't want to talk to you again. You broke a trust." That's what I heard she did with Bruce Springsteen, too. Somebody told me. He punched her out on the stage. Every time I met someone like that, the urge to withdraw grew greater. It seemed safer not getting too involved with anyone. They ultimately disappointed me, and sold our friendship out for the almighty dollar.

I'd occasionally find girls that I liked. I'd have short romances. I wasn't good at relationships. I never treated them badly. I just said, "My life is too complicated now; I have too many other things." A lot of them wanted more. I tried gently to just say it's not happening. I couldn't let them get too close. I couldn't trust anymore.

Sex alleviated some of the frustrations of life on the road. It was all: go to the stage, go back to your hotel room, go to the next town and repeat. I didn't drink, take drugs, or even eat a lot. What else could I do except the old humpty? That was my attitude. We lived on brown rice and tetracycline, which was intended to fight my acne and any venereal diseases I might pick up. You still wanna be a rock-and-roll star, eh?

More and more, I felt resentful of the merchandising, the records, the television show, the posters, the pictures, the magazines. I came to feel that that guy, that Keith Partridge/David Cassidy composite everybody was responding to, wasn't me.

I started to hate the David Cassidy the public saw. I thought, *Look what they've created. They've created this crass pop-out, this transparent, shallow, sweet, innocent, goody-goody who's now selling cornflakes.* I began to lose perspective about my positive impact on other people and how much that meant.

I had actually been a very positive, happy person when I went into this—I always felt that what the public responded to in me, even more than my looks and voice, were the intangibles I projected—but I was becoming embittered. I wanted people to know that I was very different from all of the propaganda. I looked so sweet and innocent. Yeah, right. I wanted to pull my dick out and say, "See! I am really a *bad boy*!"

Rolling Stone gave me the chance.

I was happy I'd be given a chance to really speak, to let people see the real me. I liked the idea of being profiled in a serious, respected rock journal, rather than just another cheesy teenybopper fan thing.

I agreed to give the *Rolling Stone* writer virtually unrestricted access to me. She recorded whatever she saw. If she came to my house to interview me and Sam was sunning himself, naked, she noted that; I wasn't hiding anything. If she saw bimbos trying to put moves on me, she noted that. And I didn't stop her from talking with the women around me, either, at least one of whom told her I was good in bed. If she saw a half-empty bottle of booze in my room, or smelled pot in the air, she noted all that, too. She said she wanted it to be an honest piece. The booze and the pot weren't mine. Just to keep it honest.

I spoke openly about who I was and what I wanted. I told her of my frustrations at being pigeonholed as this white-bread pop singer for prepubescent girls. That I was actually a direct contradiction to my public image. I acknowledged I didn't have any meaningful, committed, long-term relationship with a woman. I answered whatever she asked about.

Then, after we'd finished all the interviews, *Rolling Stone* requested that I do some photo shoots with Annie Leibovitz. They'd be nude shots but very tasteful, I was assured; maybe they'd show a hint of pubic hair or something, but nothing more graphic. The photos would simply reinforce the idea that in my interviews I'd had nothing to hide. I liked the idea. Annie Leibovitz was the best photographer in that genre. I thought—and still think—that the photographs she took of me were great. Revealing and real.

Maybe too real for the masses in 1972 America. I hadn't envisioned what the combined impact of the nude photos and the equally revealing interview would be. Nor had I envisioned the tone the writer would take. She wasn't greatly impressed by me.

The article created tremendous controversy. I'm sure there were plenty of mothers who never actually saw a copy of *Rolling Stone* in their life, who were telling each other over coffee or games of bridge, or at PTA get-togethers, that David Cassidy (scandal of scandals) had exposed himself, posing nude for a notorious *Rolling Stone* article, and had admitted to all kinds of debauchery.

The Partridge Family was damned near to the last gasp of real innocence on TV; there were no references to social problems of any kind on the show. Thirty-eight percent of *The Partridge Family*'s viewers were children. Many people seemed to feel I'd violated a trust with young America by letting myself be photographed naked, or be associated with booze and pot; that I was supposed to be some role model for all American youth.

I never wanted to be a role model. But even so, I must say I was very much bothered myself by the writer's implication that I smoked pot. I've admitted in this book that I tried *everything* as a teenager, from heroin, cocaine, and LSD on down—but at the time of the *Rolling Stone* article I was not using any illegal drugs. And the writer *knew* that, but chose to take the low road; she violated my trust. The pot she'd smelled wasn't mine; she knew that.

I would hardly have thought the article's suggestion that at age twenty-two I had a sex life would shock anybody. But surprise, surprise, it did. The article was written in such a vague way that different readers drew different inferences about me. The writer Dennis Cooper, who I'm sure is no dummy—his book *The Tenderness of the Wolves* was nominated for a *Los Angeles Times* Book Prize— concluded (and expressed in print) that Cassidy "as much as came out" as a homosexual in *Rolling Stone*. Of course I'd done nothing of the kind. But I can see how someone could have reached such a conclusion upon reading that I didn't have a meaningful, long-term relationship with any one woman, and that my roommate was sunning himself nude while I was being interviewed. Other readers, of course, could (and did) just as easily draw another inference— that I was living some sort of hippie lifestyle, and that if I wasn't involved in any deep, lasting relationship with any *one* woman, I was presumably involved in casual relationships with many. After all, *Rolling Stone* even quoted one woman on my supposed sexual prowess. But heterosexual promiscuity was no more acceptable than homosexuality to the "family values" crowd. The fundamental message was the same: *David Cassidy is not at all who we've all been led to believe he was*. And the last thing a performer wants to do is lose the audience's trust.

Coca-Cola changed its mind about a David Cassidy TV special they had been planning to sponsor. Up until the *Rolling Stone* article, they'd felt I was as wholesome as mom, apple pie, and Coke. Now they no longer wanted to be associated with me. General Mills threatened to stop using me. And the new, serious-rock fans I'd hoped to win by speaking frankly in the respected *Rolling Stone* magazine never materialized; I wondered if I'd ever be able to get older, hard-core music fans to take me seriously.

Ruth cautioned me that I had to be very careful about missteps. I couldn't afford any more blunders like the *Rolling Stone* story and photos. That one was my call, not hers. I felt totally spun out.

Ruth, as always, had a solution for my problems. God, how I depended on that woman. She was, I thought, a lifesaver.

She introduced me to a special doctor. She assured me he could work miracles. His clientele included a lot of stars. He exuded confidence. Anxiety could be removed instantly. He had pills for everything. He decided that in my case, the drug of choice was Valium, which he prescribed like a vitamin. I remember him telling me as I prepared for my 1983 overseas tour, "Before you leave for Europe, you should always have enough Valium." And he made sure I had plenty of it, and then plenty of other drugs he thought I needed. "They're a necessity."

The last year of *The Partridge Family*, he got me taking twenty and then forty milligrams of Valium a day. It would help my acne, he said. I'd wake up in the morning, go to work, and take a Valium. Then another after lunch. And perhaps another "as needed." I felt all right doing this, because the medication was being prescribed for me. And Ruth assured me he was a great doctor. So I didn't worry about it initially. After all, he was doing this sort of thing for a lot of big celebrities. And I clearly needed the Valium. It wasn't like I was addicted or anything, I told myself.

And there I was, so proud that I was steering clear of all illegal drugs. And seeing this doctor-to-the-stars who was the pill pusher of all time. Everybody who saw him wound up with Valium, Seconal, Quaaludes, and everything else. I remember him giving me a hundred Quaaludes, saying, "Here, these will help you sleep." Yeah, with a hundred Quaaludes you could get a lot of sleep. And a lot of rock-and-roll sex, too!

He wasn't doing anything illegal. But there seemed to be something wrong about the whole thing. He insisted we get our prescriptions filled by one particular pharmacist. We all did what we were told. My dad and Shirley, too.

On my 1973 European tour I had my own ninety-nine-passenger Caravelle jet the whole time. There's something satisfying about simply knowing you've achieved that level of success and power. For my guys, making the trip was like one big party. For me, the concerts were repetitious.

Variety reported that although my records were selling quite well throughout Europe, my planned concert appearances near Frankfurt, Germany, had to be canceled because of poor ticket sales; they pointed out that that was one region in which *The Partridge Family* was not televised, raising the question of how viable an attraction I'd be if I didn't have the TV show buoying me. Not that I worried much about that, with the screams ringing in my ears every night, and my roadies having no trouble pulling chicks for me.

The British press made a big fuss over the fact that the Queen of England invited me to lunch. I mean, all these English people are like, "Oh, ah, the Queen!" And I'm like, "The Queen?? I don't care about the Queen. The Queen means nothing to me. I think the monarchy is a joke. What makes her the Queen? Well, she waves, and she's the richest person in the world. Well, good for her. I'm rich, too. And I'd much rather meet Eric Clapton."

I figured it would have been the dullest and most strained lunch imaginable, and I had no time for that. So I canceled the Queen. No offense was intended. Although the press could not understand that.

I have to tell you, I have no regrets about having stood the Queen up. Why? Because that was the day I met Sue Shifrin for lunch. She was an artist on the same record label I was on, a singer/

songwriter, and she was a fan of mine. She came to one of my Wembley concerts. She was invited by my minder, Billy Francis, to hang out with me. The day I was supposed to be meeting the Queen, I was starting a little affair with Sue. At the time, neither of us had any idea of the significance of our getting together. Soon I would be back in America, while Sue would remain in England. (Although she's an American, she chose to live in England for nine years.) After that brief affair we became friends and eventually we both went on to other relationships, and in fact married other people. But we had a special connection from the start. And thirteen years after that first meeting—which would never have occurred if I had done the conventional thing and had lunch with the Queen— Sue would become a very important part of my life. She is now my wife.

I was on the front page of the papers every single day of this tour because I took a whole press corps with me on my plane. One journalist felt things had really gotten out of hand when even the *Times*—England's newspaper of record—considered it newsworthy that I'd caught a cold.

There were reports that I'd broken out into a "rash"—the recurring stress-related acne problem that Valium was supposed to alleviate but did not. And that I balked at requests that I sing certain songs, saying I'd recorded them months before and didn't know the words anymore.

Some reporters noted that both Sam and I visibly tensed when we saw groups of young fans approaching. One reporter quoted Sam as saying: "People think we're strange when they see us get scared of little girls, but those young ladies are terrifying. Individually they're fine, but in a crowd they get ferocious, particularly the young ones. . . . I don't know what the answer is, but I *have* managed to find a way of dealing with them at concerts. I just run!!"

The fans' intensity could get frightening, and some of my security people were really learning their business as we went along. My head of security had never been involved with anything of this magnitude before. (He went on to handle tours for some of the biggest names in the business, but he was cutting his first teeth with me.) None of the high-spirited young fans who packed our big concerts on this tour—and periodically rampaged—got seriously injured. But at least one commentator felt that that was due more to luck than anything else, and raised a cautionary note for the future.

Tony Palmer, pop music critic of the *Observer*, declared (March 25, 1973), "The disorder caused by the rampaging fanlets was often due indirectly to administrative bungling on the part of the tour's management. Both the road manager and Cassidy's personal assistant were California law students with little or no qualifications for organizing such a quasi-military operation as a pop tour. The singer's manager, Miss Ruth Aarons, is an ex-ping-pong world champion. Her 22-year-old girl assistant was, until recently, a psychiatrist's assistant. The head of Cassidy's record company once worked in production control for a motor car firm until he decided that pop music was his true vocation. . . . The English promoter who had spent six months setting up the tour did not receive a signed contract from Miss Aarons until half an hour before the first show at Wembley—already halfway through the English tour. Little wonder, therefore, that the whole fandango got out of hand."

Perhaps we should have taken note of Palmer's concern. But by the time his words saw print, we were winging our way back to the States.

CHAPTER 16

It became apparent in the fall of 1973 that in the U.S. (but not abroad) the David Cassidy/*Partridge Family* craze was over. The show's ratings, along with record sales for both David Cassidy and the Partridge Family, fell off precipitously as we went into our show's fourth and final season.

What happened? We were still a national favorite throughout our third season (1972–73). We were tied with *The Waltons* as the nineteenth most popular show on the air that season. That represented a slight drop from the previous season (which was our strongest), when we'd been rated sixteenth, but we were still in the top twenty. However, throughout the 1973–74 season, we were way down in the ratings. In January of 1974 the esteemed television critic who went by the pseudonym of "Cyclops" noted in the *New York Times* that there were only a couple of shows *less* popular than

The Partridge Family and it was inevitable that the show would be canceled—a fact, he added, that caused him genuine sorrow, since *The Partridge Family* was one of the few shows that a whole family, from the little children to parents and grandchildren, could enjoy together. (As our demise became inevitable, a number of critics confessed they'd found much to enjoy in our show.)

We faced significantly tougher competition in our last season. ABC changed our time slot from 8:30 Friday night to 8 Saturday night, putting us directly against the most popular show on the air, *All in the Family.* Ouch! That hurt.

Our cast was also aging. Our very youngest cast members were growing too old for very young viewers to identify with anymore. Screen Gems tried to combat that by introducing a new, very young kid to our cast (the traditional solution employed by family shows after a few seasons), but that didn't work. Little Ricky Segall, playing Ricky Stevens, seemed too obvious an add-on. Danny Bonaduce, as a teenager, simply wasn't as cute as he'd been as a wise-cracking little kid; things he could have said or done that would have seemed amusingly impish when he was ten could somehow seem irritating at thirteen or fourteen.

At twenty-three, my face caked in three layers of makeup, I made a less convincing teenager than ever. The fan magazines made much the same fuss over my twenty-third birthday, in April of 1973, as they had over my twenty-second and twenty-first, but the space was just a bit reduced, and the headline one of them ran, "Naturally You've Changed," tacitly acknowledged that I was approaching the upper age limit for inclusion in a magazine designed to fulfill the fantasies of young girls.

Many of those prepubescent girls who'd had crushes on me had outgrown me by our fourth year; they were now old enough to be going out on dates themselves rather than sitting at home on a Friday or Saturday night, watching TV.

And frankly, by the fourth season I was burned-out. From the show and from the whole teen-idol thing. The pills, I eventually came to realize, weren't helping me, either. The doctor said they would help me sleep and would relieve my nerves, and they did help in those areas. But I became strung out on Valium. I was becoming lethargic. I would take them in the morning and again during the day, trying to curb the anxiety and the tension I felt. After a couple of months, I was taking two blue ten-milligram Valiums a day.

Without saying anything to anyone about it, I decided to give up the Valium. I got into meditation for a while—the influence of my friend Steve Ross—attempting to heal my worn-out nerves in a more natural way. Sam and Steve and I would also fast one day a week, which we felt was healthy for the mind and body. We'd listen to Indian music and try to glean wisdom of Eastern philosophies.

But kicking the Valium, I found, didn't make all that big a difference in my life. I'd simply had enough of everything—the show, the hysteria, the road, everything. The producers knew I had no interest anymore. The last year of doing the show, I just couldn't wait for it to be over; I wanted to try to distance myself from the whole deal. I considered the whole manufactured Keith Partridge/ David Cassidy image to be one enormous pain in the ass.

As an actor, I certainly no longer had the respect of my peers. Hell, I didn't even have the respect of my own father! In an interview he gave George Maksian of New York's *Daily News* (February 10, 1974), headlined, "Cassidy Calls Son 'Bubble Gum Star,'" Maksian asked my father if he'd object if any of his other sons—Shaun, fifteen; Patrick, twelve; or Ryan, eight—followed my footsteps. My father answered: "Sure, some of the boys could follow David, the bubble gum star. But he can be used up and sucked up very fast in this business. . . . The world is full of xeroxes. But if they really have a need for it, I wouldn't stop them. My main concern is that they're really decent people. I care about what they are, and how they deal with other people." Maksian wrote that as they spoke, my father sounded envious of my success. To me, it was as if my father was attacking me in print.

I wasn't happy with my career myself. I knew it had really fucked me up, changed me. You can't go through those things and come out the other side without being different. I hated the pressure of being an idol, of feeling I was expected to be a superstar onstage and a superhuman offstage. After four years of "stardom," I just couldn't talk to people anymore. The Partridge Family/teen-idol trip had distorted people's perception of me and my own perception of me so much that I didn't like what I'd become. I was a serious actor when I started, when I made my initial guest appearances on television. I don't think anyone has ever taken me seriously as an actor in the years since *The Partridge Family*. I can't shake that albatross around my neck. As we filmed the final season of *The Partridge Family*, I'd sometimes feel deep regrets for the direction I'd chosen. I'd think, *I could have become a respected, working actor, like my dad had wanted. But thanks to this damned Partridge Family/rock star identity I've acquired, people never will accept me as a serious actor. I've got to get off this friggin' bus!*

The only way out that I could see was to simply quit show business entirely. Ruth certainly didn't want to hear of such talk— not just for my sake, I'm sure, but for hers. After all, I had become her major breadwinner; if I retired, she stood to lose a considerable source of income. From her point of view, it was foolish of me to think of retirement. Demand for me on the concert circuit was strong and would likely remain strong for quite some time. Maybe years still. Record companies and producers still had confidence in me; it was silly to talk of quitting.

The Partridge Family's first five albums, released within less than two years, had all gone gold. The first three had made it to the Top 10 on the *Billboard* charts. But the Family's sixth album, *The Partridge Family Notebook*, showed signs of decline. I begged the record company to change the sound. And the Family's seventh album, *Crossword Puzzle*, which made the charts for just five weeks in the summer of 1973, was only a mild success. It was the last Partridge Family album to make the charts at all, and none of their singles were becoming hits anymore, either. Throughout the 1973–74 television season the Partridge Family, for the first time in its history, was without a hit record. It just refused to change with the times. I wanted out.

What was the point in making more records like those I'd made? The public clearly wasn't interested in them anymore. How can you keep making the same record over and over and keep expecting success? This drove me crazy. I lost a lot of sleep over it.

I knew what I wanted to do. Deciding to quit was not a difficult decision for me. I told Ruth I'd fulfill the obligations I had; I'd finish the fourth TV season, make the records I was required to, do one last huge world concert tour, and then quit while I could still say I was on top.

As American newspapers reported that the David Cassidy/ Partridge Family mania was receding into history, manufacturers quietly stopped renewing licensing agreements; they figured they'd marketed about as many units of Partridge Family bubble gum and David Cassidy beach towels as they were going to. Chuck Laufer changed the publication schedule of his *Partridge Family Magazine* from monthly to bimonthly, to quarterly, then killed it.

The longer I remained in the spotlight, the more I believed it antagonized my father and made him resent me. I really wanted his love. So in addition to all the other good reasons I had for quitting, I imagined that it also might bring my father and me closer together. He could be the undisputed star of the family. I would never again upstage him. I felt better, once I'd made up my mind to get out. And it looked to me like the timing was just right. I'd be quitting while I was still on top. No one would outdraw my last concert tour.

My records were actually selling better than ever in England. I'd started later in England than in the U.S. It was only logical, I supposed, that I would last longer there. The British fans really took to me in a way that was gratifying.

In October of 1973 I topped the British charts for several weeks with a single combining "Daydreamer" and "The Puppy Song" (neither of which were hits in the U.S.). In December of '73 my album *Dreams Are Nothin' More Than Wishes* became the number-one album in England, and in the summer of '74 I had two hit singles on the British charts, "If I Didn't Care" (peaking at 9) and a revival of the Beatles' "Please, Please Me" (peaking at 16), plus one hit album, *Cassidy Live* (peaking at 9)—none of which made a ripple in the U.S. In England I was more popular than I'd ever been, the year I decided to quit. I felt good about that. I wasn't going to overstay my welcome.

My routine continued pretty much as normal. I'd do the TV show weekdays. I'd record at night. On weekends I'd tour. And on Monday mornings I'd be back at the set, telling Susan how the security guards had had to hide me in the trunk of a car so I could escape my frenzied fans; how many chicks I'd had sex with; how frustrating it was for me that I couldn't form any kind of meaningful relationship with a woman. I'd moan a lot to Susan, who seemed to understand so perfectly, how I never seemed to meet any good-looking, bright, caring, sensitive women who I could really connect with, women with whom a genuine, lasting relationship might be possible. Where could I ever find such a woman? How come they were in such short supply? Susan would listen understandingly.

CHAPTER
17

Y̶ou've got to be careful about Susan," Shirley said to me one day.

I said, "What are you talking about?"

"You've got to be careful how you talk around her, about all
of the other women in your life. You don't want to hurt her."

"Huh? What do you mean?"

So I had sex with a lot of chicks; so I wasn't serious about
them; so I talked about these things with Susan. Susan knew me
well. She was the sister I'd never had. I just couldn't imagine how
my talking openly about sex or anything else could hurt Susan. I
didn't get what Shirley was driving at. I was so blind, I probably
ought to have Shirley let you in on what was going on.

"Susan had a giant crush on David," Shirley recalls. "She was
just mad about him—just gaga over him. And David didn't see it

coming. They were friends first. They worked together and confided in one another, throughout the years that she was involved with Dale. It was over a long period of time that her feelings for David developed. He wasn't aware of it at all. Susan would say things to me and make little hints about it."

Finally, Shirley prodded me directly: "David, you really ought to look at Susan." Beat, beat, beat. "*Look* at Susan?"

I was surprised. "What are you talking about? She's Susan! You know, my sister, Susan!"

One night, just after the final wrap party for *The Partridge Family*, I took Susan out to dinner. We were now through with the show for good; the cast members were all moving off in different directions. I just wanted to have dinner with her and keep our friendship alive. I knew I'd be going on a world tour shortly and then retiring from the business for the foreseeable future. Susan didn't know where she'd be working next. Maybe that sense of things coming to an end helped draw us closer together.

After dinner, we went by my old high school. We talked about the past years, from when we'd first met when she was a fifteen-year-old just trying out for the show. We both started weeping. She told me in great detail—we must have spent three hours sitting there—how long she had loved me and how difficult it had been for her, and how afraid she was of what was going to happen with our future. I felt like such a dumb fuck. It was as if she had hit me over the head with a baseball bat.

We'd grown so close. And when Susan told me about all the times she had wanted to really be with me and how difficult it had been to just silently listen to me go on and on about *my* experiences, and *my* achy-breaky heart—that had a lot of impact on me.

When I needed to get away, I used to go down to Rancho California, in San Diego County, where our director of photography had a ranch. It was a sanctuary for me. Susan told me she'd like to go down with me to the ranch the next time I went. I said all right.

But it really felt awkward. I valued this person and her friendship and her love. Aren't we taught the best thing your mate could be is your best friend? Susan was certainly one of my best friends, my best female friend. But there are some people toward whom— as soon as you meet them—you feel an animal attraction; you just want to have sex with them. The truth is, I guess I never felt that way with Susan. I thought she was really attractive. But sexually— I never had that hunger for her. I never thought, as I had with various others, *I've got to have that ass.*

When we got to the ranch, I kept thinking, *Susan's looking at me like, "Let's go to bed."* I made small talk about horse racing, one of my favorite subjects, sort of beating around the bush. Then we decided to watch some TV. Eventually we started making out, kissing and hugging; I figured that was what we had come down for. I thought, *Okay, here I am, I'm actually kissing her now. And I guess what's going to happen next is I'm going to start taking her clothes off, which is weird.* My dick was getting hard, but I was thinking something like, *My sister here is attractive, but do I really want to fuck my sister?* Even though, of course, Susan was not a blood relative, that's how I'd come to think of her.

She went into the bathroom to brush her teeth and get ready for bed. I sat in bed thinking, *Okay, she's in the bathroom. Is there some way I can get out of this? Or should I just go for it?* I thought, *If I don't have sex with her, she's going to believe I don't find her attractive.* Which was the last thing I wanted her to feel. So I told myself, *Just have sex with her. She wants you to. If you fuck this situation up, you're going to fuck your whole relationship up.* Oh, shit! It's always been so easy with any other woman. What if we wake tomorrow and regret it? Oh, no.

When Susan got back in the room, wearing just her underwear, we turned off the lights and lay down on the bed, clearly ready for me to make my move. But Susan lacked the slutty aspect of a female that I always found so attractive. She was never going to say, "I want to take that big piece of meat of yours, baby." To me she wasn't dirty. She wasn't nasty. She was good.

So, I felt, *I just can't win. I'm damned if I fuck her and I'm damned if I don't. If I don't do it, she's going to resent the shit out of me. And if I do, it'll ruin the good relationship as friends that we've had. Why did she have to put me in this spot? Why couldn't we have just left things the way they've always been between us?* What do I do? Comedy . . . yeah, so I started telling jokes and fucking around in bed, to sort of break the tension. Then we started making out, and I wound up lying all over her. Then I told her I was really tired—too tired to do anything more—but I really felt good lying there with her; I felt connected. I fell asleep. I was postponing the inevitable.

In the morning, having sex with her seemed so much more plausible. I woke up with an erection. I was like, *Well, I'm half-asleep and I'm not really thinking clearly any longer*. And we had a sort of semi-aborted sexual experience that I've tried to black out of my mind. Here I was, trying to give someone I loved something I knew she wanted, and realizing, in the process, it was not what *I* really wanted. She started to sense my ambivalence. I think she probably felt like she wasn't that attractive to me, which was probably the worst thing I could have done, especially since she was sort of insecure about her looks. I mean, if a woman doesn't feel attractive to someone, I don't think there's anything you can do that can cut them more deeply than reject them in bed. So what occurred was a brief sexual encounter that was pretty unsuccessful, pretty unfulfilling for us both. And without my wanting it to happen, Susan felt rejected by me. We've never discussed it. It's been twenty years now. But that changed us forever.

If I couldn't give Susan the love she seemed to want from me,

I did give her all of the show business help I could, which was also something she wanted. I connected her with people who'd been guiding my career, whom I believed could help her get the work she wanted. And they did. Ruth Aarons, whom I'd told Susan was as powerful and clever as any manager in the business, became Susan's manager and saw to it that Susan was soon signed to another TV show. My agent at the William Morris Agency, Lenny Hirshan, took a strong interest in Susan both professionally and personally. Eventually Lenny and Susan married. Susan actually went on to have the most successful post–*Partridge Family* acting career of all of us. I took it for granted that Susan and I would always be very close friends; I knew her about as well as anyone did. And for some years afterward, we did periodically connect with one another again.

Don't ask me what's happened between Susan and me in more recent years, though, because I honestly don't know. We just don't talk at all anymore. Communications were terminated from her end, not mine. I saw her a couple of months ago and it was warm but brief. No talk of a future. Only a past.

I still love Susan in some special way. I can never let that go.

CHAPTER
18

The last world tour turned out to be a circus. We were all partying hard—the band, the security people, everybody—just blowing off steam before we packed it all in for good. If you ask me what I remember from that tour, the hijinks and escapades come to mind before any of the concerts themselves.

That trip was a free-flying sexual circus. Three sexually incredible Dutch stewardesses were provided with the private jet we chartered in Europe. Someone must have handpicked those girls for us. They came back to the hotel rooms with us, and we all took turns with them. They partied with everyone. And when it was time for them to do their regular jobs on board the jet, they were thoroughly professional.

I remember hanging around with Gina Lollobrigida, the Italian sex goddess—who was about twice my age but very attractive—

over a period of several days in Australia. The first time she met me she said, "I hear you're a monster. I want to meet the monster." And she looked down at my crotch. She said she was doing a photo book—she'd gotten into photography after retiring from the screen—and asked me to pose for her.

She came up to my suite with her camera. She ordered up $200 worth of grapes, bananas, and other fruit, and said, "I want you to take all your clothes off, get into bed, drape the sheet around you." She went in the other room. I took my clothes off, got into the bed, and said, "Okay." She came in and began to move the sheet down and arrange the grapes and bananas, which turned me on. She was slowly moving this fruit around and she saw that I'd gotten an erection. I'll never forget the look on her face when she lifted the sheet up—it was really comic. She was laughing, crying: "Oh, my God." She was pretty funny. I liked her. And I'm glad she included me in her book (along with Henry Kissinger and some other pretty interesting men she'd known).

I played the Melbourne Cricket Grounds to 65,000 people. I was the last performer to play there until Paul McCartney in 1993, nineteen years later. Gina Lollobrigida introduced me to the audience, which I really got a kick out of—even though I'm sure my younger fans probably didn't even know who she was.

I remember this one attractive woman fan of about twenty-five who got it on with me while we were in Japan. I had the Presidential Suite at the Tokyo Hilton—about thirteen rooms for me and my inner sanctum, the guys I lived with and traveled with, like Billy Francis, Sam, and Steve. I met this woman in the hall; she was shacking up with some older ambassador whose room was across the way. We chatted. I gave her an autographed picture, that sort of thing.

So the next night she came knocking on my door at about one in the morning.

"Come on in," I said.

"Oh, I can't. He's gone to sleep. I just snuck out. I wanted to come and see you," she said.

"I'm glad you did."

"Oh, he's married, you see. I'm just here with him." She told me about the older guy I'd seen her with.

"Really?"

I'd been out in the hall earlier and I'd overheard her arguing with the guy in their room. He didn't want her flirting with me; she told him I was her idol, and she just wanted to meet me. I knew what that meant.

I was sitting casually on the bed, chatting with her, wearing only a towel that I'd slipped around my waist to answer the door. I let the towel drop. I said, "Look, would you like to stay for a while?"

"I believe I will." She came over to the bed, began taking her clothes off, and pushed her body up next to me. Then abruptly, panicking, she said, "But I've got to go. We're leaving tomorrow at eleven A.M."

"Okay, good night," I said, not pressing the issue at all. She ran back to her ambassador friend. I guess she'd worried that the guy might wake up and find she'd snuck out.

In the morning there was a knock on my door. I put a towel around my waist, cracked the door, saw that it was her, and let her in.

"Look, I've got to catch a plane," she said as she started taking her clothes off, "but I absolutely have to have you." She jumped into bed. She lay on top of me, facing the headboard, very passionate. She was obviously turned on, going, "Oh, oh, oh . . ." Well, my guys must have heard her. They started coming through the doors of the suite that led into my bedroom. She was so deeply into it, she didn't even seem to notice them come in.

They sat down on chairs in my room, enjoying what amounted to a matinee performance for them.

By this point the girl was really howling, in the heat of passion, flipping. She's reaching orgasm. Finally, as she was really going at it on top of me—seemingly lost in ecstasy—she raised one arm and glanced at her watch, to make sure she wasn't staying too late. Then back to the screaming! At that point, my guys lost it. They burst out laughing and just blew it.

She turned around, muttered, "Oh, fuck it," and continued until she finished. Then she said, "You're absolutely fantastic. I think you're the most incredible person I've ever known." She dressed and rushed out the door, saying, "Bye, love you." I'd known her maybe a total of seven minutes. My guys stood and gave me an ovation. Juvenile, did I say? Nah.

I took maybe twenty-five of my own people with me as we toured, plus maybe twenty-five members of the press. I played for audiences of 20,000, 40,000, 60,000 people. And beat though I was—by the last concerts of the tour I felt totally burned-out, totally exhausted—when I'd hit the stage, the crowd would give me instant energy. There's a certain sense of power, too, communicating with tens of thousands of people. If you shout out, "I think I love you," you'll get countless shouts of "I love you" back. If you reach out, as if trying to make contact, tens of thousands of fans will move, as if drawn, toward you.

After a few hundred fans got hurt at one of my Australian shows, a government official declared me a hazard to public health. I was thinking like, *Hey, lighten up; we're just trying to give everybody a little entertainment*. It wasn't as if mine were the first rock concerts at which anyone had ever gotten hurt. That goes with the territory. But to a significant portion of the press, I became this villain who'd brought mayhem to tranquil Australia, like it was my fault that all these kids had to be treated by the ambulance corps. The press called it pandemonium. And that started to get to me, seeing the way the press could manipulate to make me look bad. The way the press could turn on you—that was another reason I was glad I'd be getting out of the game soon.

The final stop on my tour was England. I remember what a thrill it was for me to finally meet Paul McCartney. I'd met John Lennon, of course, but I'd never met Paul. Steve Ross and I went to see Paul in his new band, Wings. They ran through their whole show, giving us in effect a private concert, as they rehearsed in this huge, otherwise deserted sound stage. Afterward, we got up onstage and jammed with them.

I played three huge stadiums in Scotland and England—the type of places the Beatles had played, but no one else was playing. So that in itself guaranteed massive press attention. And don't forget, my records were high on the British charts in May of 1974; I arrived like a conquering hero. Approaching Glasgow, my first stop, the fans lined the road from the airport for miles, giving me the kind of reception they'd ordinarily give royalty.

Then I played White City Stadium in London; there were 40,000 fans inside and perhaps as many more outside. Fans were not just in the bleachers; we had them packed standing on the field, too—more seating had been provided for those down there. The fans went wild. I kept saying, "Get back, get back, you've got to stop pushing! They're going to stop the show, they're going to pull the plug on me. You've got to maintain—cool it!" But when you tell people who are that worked up, "Stop going berserk," they only go further overboard. I was trying to tell them, "If you don't stop, I'm off the stage. You've got to move back." I don't even know if they could hear me.

There was gridlock outside the stadium, there were so many cars there. Cars were parked six deep. I never had a harder time making a getaway. My security guys told me a lot of girls had fainted and some had been taken to the hospital, but I had no idea how severe it was. We always anticipated some fans would faint, due to all the excitement. We had first-aid people standing by. But I could already anticipate the press making me out to be the heavy, as they had in Australia, because the crowd at my White City Stadium concert had gotten so out of control.

A few nights later, I gave my very last concert, in Manchester, England, where the crowd—knowing it was my absolute farewell show—made more noise than any I'd ever heard. I had to stuff my ears with cotton. I had a Marshall amp turned all the way up to 10, to try to project over all of the screaming. I could barely hear anything I was doing. That was an amazing night. The crowd gave me so much energy. I remember running off the stage, running across the field after the final number. Then I came back and said, "I love you, it's been incredible. You're not going to see me for a while, but someday I'll be back. I just want you to know how much it's meant to me." Then I sang for an encore "It's All Over Now, Baby Blue."

I ran the whole length of the field into a waiting car, while 40,000 people were screaming and crying. I left happily, but with a sense of disbelief. I mean, after four years, to walk out of the stadium with that crowd of people screaming for me and to know I'm never going to do this again.

It was time, I felt, definitely time. I breathed a giant sigh of relief, a sense of *Thank God I made it*.

One of my fans, unfortunately, did not come through alive. Bernadette Whelan, a fourteen-year-old British schoolgirl, was fatally injured at my White City Stadium concert. She was among those taken from the stadium by ambulance to a nearby hospital, where she managed to linger for four days before dying. I had no idea, the night I gave my final concert, that at White City Stadium one of my fans had been carried out in a coma.

Her passing received extensive coverage. The press, which would otherwise have focused attention on my retirement, understandably focused instead on her tragic death, casting a pall over my whole concert career. At the time, I was very unhappy and upset over the coverage, feeling I was being unfairly blamed for a young girl's death. I couldn't even bring myself to read all the things that were written, they were so painful. My people assured me repeatedly that we had in no way been responsible for Bernadette's death. They told me that she had gone to the concert with known heart problems; everyone understood that her health was not good; and that she suffered a heart attack during the excitement of my concert. But, in reviewing newspaper coverage of the event in preparation for this book, I realize that what I was told by my people about her death— what I've always found comforting to believe—was simply not true.

For one thing, the government held a formal inquest into her death, which would not have been done had her doctor reported she had died from a routine heart attack. The *Times* of London, a newspaper unsurpassed in terms of objectivity, accuracy, and fairness, reported on June 18, 1979, that at the inquest concerning Bernadette Whelan's death, "Dr. Rufus Compton, a pathologist, said the girl died of traumatic asphyxia. Obstruction of respiration was mainly a result of compression of the body. Her brain had been damaged by cardiac arrest." In layman's terms, she had been crushed to death by the crowd. Her father, the *Times* reported, testified that the girl had gone to the concert "in perfectly good health." He received word some time later that she'd been taken by ambulance to Hammersmith Hospital. According to the *Times*, "St. John Ambulance workers dealt with 500 casualties, and 30 people were taken to the hospital."

Hammersmith coroner Dr. John Burton testified that 10,000 young fans had been "crowded up against a barrier in the center of the arena, with no means of getting out," in a highly charged situation, with hysteria spreading through the crowd. Burton cautioned those attending the inquest that he was going to play a tape recording of a twenty-minute portion of the concert which was so disturbing that some people might want to leave. On the tape, girls could be heard shouting, "Please get me out," while loudspeaker appeals were made in vain for the crowd to stop pressing forward.

Disc jockey Tony Blackburn, who had served as an emcee at the concert, testified that he had never before seen so many people removed from a concert on stretchers; nor had he seen a concert before mine at which seating had not been provided for everybody.

I certainly did not want to believe that I could in any way have been responsible for the death of one of my fans. I still to this day believe that I and my security did everything we could to keep my fans safe. However, had you seen the thousands of fans pushing hysterically toward the stage that night, you would have concluded as I had: you simply can't contain teenage girls who are out of control with their emotions. We did everything we could but failed.

CHAPTER
19

The years from my retirement in May of 1974, at the age of twenty-four, up through about 1980 were the darkest I'd ever known.

When I retired, I suffered a breakdown—or several successive breakdowns, it felt like, because each time I thought I'd fallen as low as I could go, the bottom would drop out from under me again.

For the first six months I literally locked myself in my room. I sat alone, talking to myself, trying to figure out what the fuck had happened. I can't remember a whole lot about that period. I just remember feeling bleak. Empty. I increasingly found solace in drinking. I wanted to anesthetize myself. I was so lost.

The pain I was trying to numb was rooted in the reality that the kind of career I'd wanted, I didn't have. And the career I'd had, I never wanted. Sure, I still had plenty of fans. But did they love *me* or just the image of me, which had been totally manufactured and marketed? I thought I'd like to sing songs that truly expressed who I was. But who was I? I hadn't a clue. And would the fans have any interest in the real me, anyway?

I may have been twenty-four when I retired, but emotionally I was still a teenager. I regretted having ever gotten aboard that Partridge Family bus. Sure, I'd become a star. But I'd also become a trapped, stunted human being, cut off from everyone else, unable to go anywhere, unable to interact with others in a normal way. I'd lost the ability to really relate to people.

Playing that pop-star role for years had brought me to the point of ulcers. So I felt I had to find a way to rebuild and go back to the beginning of me. But how could I start over? I had no idea. The easiest course to take was to just shut down. To withdraw into my cocoon and hope that time would help me heal.

I was an insomniac to begin with and I found it getting worse. I found myself staying up later and later at night. It was a problem sleeping, and there was no joy in being awake, so I tried to dull my existence one way or another. The clean-living, hardworking vegetarian turned into this guy who was willing to try anything to take him outside himself. Cocaine, heroin, alcohol. I didn't care.

My mother saw me spinning out, drowning in my sorrows, and made a couple of attempts to intervene. I didn't want to hear it. Like a teenage brat, I'd tell her, "Leave me alone, Ma." My mother actually moved in with me for a couple of months. But that was a mistake. When you're an adult, you can't live with your mother. If I wanted to play drums at five in the morning, I wanted to play drums; I didn't want my mother saying, "Go to sleep." And I often liked to play music all through the night. I had a few musician friends I felt comfortable with, who could stay up all night with me, partying and playing. I told my mom, "This is my house. I live here. You're living here with me, but you can't tell me what to do."

I'd replay in my mind the events leading up to my quitting the business, trying to analyze what I'd done.

After I retired, my father was in the spotlight a bit more, which I hope brought him some happiness. In the last few years of his life, he got some of the best roles of his career, playing wonderfully villainous characters everywhere from *Columbo* on TV to *The Eiger Sanction* (1975) on-screen. And he particularly delighted in portraying his original idol, John Barrymore, in the film *W. C. Fields and Me* (1976).

He said he wanted to become closer to me. Maybe he was worried about what was happening to me, too; I don't know. We made a few attempts to connect, but nothing turned out the way I'd imagined it might. He went overboard. Instead of starting slow, maybe suggesting we have dinner together, he brought my brother Ryan out to my house in Encino and spent the weekend with me. He was in this *I want to get to know you, son*, mode, acting as if the three of us being together for a weekend would be great fun, like we were buddies going on some fucking camping trip. Only I'd gotten too old for camping trips and his showbiz stories. As we talked, I realized that I had nothing in common with him, except for the fact that we'd both become pretty heavy drinkers. But I didn't want to drink with my father. Or do much of anything else with him. (At one point he told me, "One thing we'll never do is share women." And I thought, naively, *Of course not*. After all, he was still married to Shirley, though he'd never hidden from me the fact that he'd cheated on her.) I couldn't wait for our weekend together to be over. There were some good moments—like we'd find ourselves just laughing together, so comfortable. Then suddenly he'd turn and say something like, "C'mon now, I'm your father." I felt I couldn't trust him any more now than I could when I was a child.

I was relieved when he finally left. And yet, at the last moment I found myself unexpectedly feeling sorry for him. I can't explain it. For the first time I really looked at him, and I told myself, *He's going to be all right*—I mean, trying to convince myself of that but unable to quite believe it. There was something frighteningly desperate in the way he was trying to hang on to a relationship with me that really wasn't there, that maybe never had been there. I'd originally thought that maybe he'd come out for a weekend for my benefit, because he was worried I was drowning, which in a way I was. But now I sensed he was having trouble staying afloat, too.

It was sometimes hard for me to reconcile the often difficult, mercurial man that I experienced Jack Cassidy to be with the popular, hearty, hail-fellow-well-met that everybody in Hollywood used to tell me he was. I must have heard it a thousand times: "Your father—what a guy!" He could radiate such charm, such wit, such personality, he could seduce the whole world. He had a certain roguish wild streak that many people found entertaining. He could get away with doing anything—things I certainly could never get away with because I deal too much in the present reality; my dad lived in his own reality. No matter what he did, his friends would just say, "Oh, well, it's just Jack!" He had such a vivid personality that still to this day people who knew him, no matter how briefly, always have stories to tell me about him.

The actor Jack Klugman, of *Odd Couple* fame, told me of how, one day in 1974, he found himself riding up in a crowded elevator in the black tower with my father at Universal Studios. When the elevator reached my dad's floor, my dad kissed Jack Klugman on the mouth and said, "You know, I'll always love you," gaily walked out, and let the elevator doors close on a startled, chagrined Klugman, who was babbling to the studio executives all around him, "I had nothing to do with that; I don't even know that person!" Klugman had never been put in a spot like that in his life, but took it with good humor as a real Jack Cassidy gag. I mean, my dad would do shit like that, mess with people, all the time. And people would keep saying, "That Jack. What a guy! What a character!"

Few knew there was also a very dark side to my father that most of his showbiz pals never saw, or pretended not to see. All of us who'd ever dealt with him intimately—my mother, Shirley, my brothers, and I—we'd instinctively tried hard to keep him happy, always tried to agree with him as much as possible, to keep that dark side from rearing its ugly head. Some people outside of the family also sensed that dark side was there and grew uncomfortable.

My dad had a wonderful relationship with James Cagney. He worshipped Cagney, he even called him "Dad," spent time at his home. They established this real bond, based on their shared Irish family roots and showbiz interests. But my dad would spin too far out. And eventually, not long before my father died, Cagney had to tell him, "I can't see you anymore. You're out of your mind." And my dad said he was through with Cagney for good. He burned up people like he burned money.

I think reality was so painful for my father, he preferred creating his own. He had such a damaging childhood—he was thoroughly rejected by his mother—perhaps it's no wonder he had so many problems as an adult. Or perhaps there was just something awry in his genes. But I felt my father had one foot in reality and one foot in his *own* reality. If you tried to challenge him about anything, tried to suggest he wasn't being rational, he'd cross you off his list. So we all in our own fashion—in order to have his love and feed his ego and make him feel good so he would make us feel good—would choose to say, "Yeah, you're right, Dad. The pink elephants in the room really do look interesting."

In some way, I never really felt I knew my dad. I don't mean just that we were estranged—we pretty much were as I grew older, and that, unfortunately, got worse in the final couple of years of his life—but also that he was always very uncomfortable about letting me know who he really was. He was very strange about sharing his real feelings, as opposed to being open and honest with me. Ultimately I learned more about his life from other people than I did from him. Ah, those stories . . .

Nothing anyone ever said or hinted about my father seemed shocking or implausible to me. He was a man who you could imagine doing almost anything, because he just wasn't like most people. I'd see that in a million little ways. Here's one small Jack Cassidy incident that comes to mind. We were sitting in a restaurant one day, perhaps 1974 or '75. He was puffing away on a cigarette, even though he was under doctor's orders not to smoke; he'd developed a node on his vocal cords. A good-looking woman walked over to our table and asked if she could borrow a cigarette.

Dad takes a big drag and says, "I'm sorry, but I don't smoke."

Amused and puzzled, she asked, "You don't smoke?"

"I've quit," he explained.

"But isn't that a cigarette you're smoking right now?" she asks.

My father, totally straight, completely convinced, says, without fear of contradiction, "Yes, but *mentally* I've quit."

That was Jack Cassidy. He believed it, he convinced himself it was okay to smoke because *mentally* he'd quit. Who was I to argue?

That madness and eccentricity went hand in hand with his being so gifted and so talented. And I don't mean just gifted and talented as an actor or a singer; he had an excellent grasp of what worked in show business generally. When he and Shirley made nightclub appearances, she may have been the one drawing the crowds (because of her movie and television fame), but he was the one who put together the acts. Although they were separated throughout 1973, they got back together again the next year. They toured for much of '74 with an act that was (as the credits read) "conceived, written, produced, and directed by Jack Cassidy."

Called "The Wedding Band—The Jack Cassidy and Shirley Jones Show," their act (which also featured supporting singers and dancers) was inspired by their courtship, marriage, separation, and reconciliation. My dad had a good eye for what worked and what didn't. And he had exquisite taste. Do you know, late in his life, he also decorated friends' storefront windows just for fun? If Hollywood ever turned its back on him, friends would joke, he could start a new career as a set decorator. I was always impressed that he had so many talents. It was actually intimidating. He could draw, sculpt, build anything artistic with his hands.

I began to worry about the way my father was acting in 1974. He seemed to be losing his grip, seemed to be coming unraveled in some general way. Maybe I should have been worrying more about myself. He didn't like my just sitting idle. He felt I had talents that should be developed. He wanted to see me working at my craft, learning. If I didn't like what I'd made of my life so far, he felt I should simply start afresh. Try something new. My father believed in the infinite possibilities of life. For that I now thank him.

Late that year I got a call, quite unexpectedly, from David Bowie. He was already doing pretty well as a performer; his career, it appeared, was just on the verge of exploding in a big way. I liked his work, particularly his album *The Rise and Fall of Ziggy Stardust and the Spiders from Mars*. People had often said I'd had an androgynous look, but Bowie took the concept of androgyny to a whole 'nother level. I was intrigued that he appreciated my work.

He told me he wanted to produce an album—me singing songs that he and others would write. He said he envisioned an album that would give me a far more adult image than I'd had through my Partridge Family years. I was intrigued enough by what he said to fly to New York, where he and his entourage were encamped at the Sherry-Netherland Hotel, and meet with him.

I found that he lived in a very subterranean–New York, avant-garde kind of world of transsexuals and transvestites. It was like a carnival at his place. There were some people in the other rooms doing mime. He had a whole bunch of people around him who, I guess, made life interesting for him, including some whom I couldn't tell the gender of—and perhaps they weren't sure either. Bowie just enjoyed feeling part of this very hip, inside, New York, artistic scene. To me it held no fascination at all. It felt false and posed.

We were at different ends of the spectrum, two guys sitting by history—one's success in the pop music field largely behind him, the other's largely in front of him. He was very enthusiastic over the next album he had coming out and all of the touring he would be doing to promote it. The album was *Diamond Dogs*. The mere thought of touring was almost repulsive to me. Even if I made the album he had in mind, there was no way I was going to go out and do concerts to promote it—which you really need to do if you want to make an album a big hit. He really craved all of the mass adulation that I'd had enough of. My own take on him was, *I don't want to be where you're headed. Been there. Done it. Thanks.*

He played me a couple of songs that he'd written, and that Lou Reed had written, for the album he wanted me to do. I just didn't think they were interesting enough. Or right for me. One was called, as I recall, "I'm All Grown Up Now"—too obvious, I thought. I said, "I like the idea. I just don't hear these songs." The proposed album never came to be. We couldn't even decide on *where* to record it.

Instead, I wound up signing a contract with RCA Records. I agreed to record again, but only if I could do material I believed in—I'd had enough compromises in my career and wanted to feature mostly my own material from now on—and only if I would not have to tour to promote my albums. I wasn't interested in touring. If I toured, I knew, the fans would expect me to do the old songs from *The Partridge Family*. I couldn't stomach that thought.

Variety had the right take when they wrote that for my RCA albums, I was dropping my "manufactured image" to offer the real me. Years later, a lot of people who'd bought those albums would come up to me and say, "They were the best ones you ever made," which I really liked hearing. I was particularly proud of the first RCA album I did, a tongue-in-cheek kind of semiautobiographical thing called *The Higher They Climb, the Harder They Fall*, about the rise and fall of a rock-and-roll star. I tried to tell a story humorously through songs about this all-American kid, who was of course me, who lives the American dream that goes wrong. People were shocked. They couldn't imagine that I could make fun of myself like that. It was the most artistic statement I'd ever made, and certainly the most honest.

My RCA albums were in the black financially, but they didn't get played much on the radio. They didn't make the charts. A couple of my RCA singles made the British charts that year—one of which was called "I Write the Songs." My recording of that song, which was the first ever of that song, was first released in the U.K. It became an instant hit for me. But a record exec for another label heard my version while on a trip to England, brought it back to the U.S., and had Barry Manilow record a cover version. It became a million-seller for Manilow, the "Record of the Year."

My RCA recordings were successful enough worldwide so that if I'd wanted to carry on and keep making records I could have, but making records just wasn't doing it for me then either. I wasn't finding any satisfaction in life. I just looked for various means of escape. I even got into gambling somewhat, which had never been my thing. (My dad was the one who'd sometimes get into trouble from gambling too much; gambling was his thing, not mine.) And a lot of the time, I'd simply stay in my room. I wasn't sure I wanted to record anymore, yet I kept composing songs the public never heard. I felt like the square peg, unable to fit in that round hole. I've found myself feeling that way many, many times in my life: that I don't quite fit.

CHAPTER
20

In late 1974 I got a call from my dad. He and Shirley, and a few supporting singers and dancers, were touring the Northeast with their show, "The Wedding Band." He wanted Shaun, Patrick, Ryan, and me to fly out and spend some time with them. They were then playing at a music theater in Massachusetts.

I remember flying across the country with my brothers because that was the first time all of us were together without either my dad or Shirley. I was the only real adult. Well, sort of. I was twenty-four, Shaun was sixteen, Patrick around fourteen, and Ryan twelve. We checked into the hotel. They told us Dad and Shirley were in the restaurant, along with James Cagney and Cagney's wife.

In the last years of his life, lots of things were going askew with my dad emotionally. He was feeling the loss of family (his calling James Cagney "Dad" was, I think, a way of making up for that). His brother Joe had died. He had severed his relationship with his sister, Gertrude, and he was kind of severing his relationship with his other brother, Willy. Anytime you tried to get my father to deal with reality, it was: "You either see it my way or else you're off the show."

Lately I'd been hearing some weird things about his behavior. Word would filter back to me. But hearing things is one thing; seeing them is another.

We entered this restaurant at this hotel in the middle of Nowhere, Massachusetts. We spotted their table: my dad was there, along with Shirley, James Cagney, and Cagney's wife, Bill. My dad stood up and ran across the room to us. Ignoring my brothers, he put his hands around my face, grabbed me, kissed me on the lips, and started to cry, saying, "Oh, thank God you cut your hair. You reminded me so much of your mother before."

I mean, "Hi, Dad! Great to see you!" My brothers were thinking, *Holy shit, what's going on?* Their mouths just fell open. It was like my dad didn't even notice my brothers; he only noticed that I'd cut my hair short. He said, "Oh God, David, I'm glad to see you again." Hugged me, standing in the middle of the room weeping.

Then he introduced me to Cagney and his wife. My brothers and I sat down at the table. And now my father got into the role of being our host. He'd stand up, he'd sit down—the nonstop talker, the entertainer, going, "And if you think that's fun, wait till you hear this." I mean, he was really *on*. He usually seemed sort of over the top anyway, but this was different. He was way over. There was some little glint in his eyes that seemed to say, not *I'm having fun tonight*, but something more like *I'm just a little bit twisted*. Like something was frying in him.

On the way to the theater, where he and Shirley were supposed to give their show that night, he pulled out a hip flask, took a swig, and said, "Let's forget about the show and go get drunk." And then, after a beat, he laughed like of course he was just kidding. Only it didn't feel like he was kidding. I knew he was close to the edge.

He continued, "I don't want to work tonight. I just want to spend it with my family."

"But, Dad, you have to go to work tonight."

"Why?"

He did the show okay. What I remember most about that weekend, though, was that I had an instant rapport with one of the girls in the show. We had dinner, went back to my room for drinks, and I did what I used to do best. In the afterglow we talked. She went on and on about what a wonderful man my father is and how she thought so highly of him, and a light went on in my head: oh, no, she's been sleeping with my father. (The next day, she confirmed that that was the case, and that my father had told her that although he and Shirley made a good team professionally, they no longer enjoyed marital relations.)

In the meantime, who should come knocking at my door but my father. It was five in the morning. I was lying in bed talking with this girl, and my father—who'd been up all night drinking (and perhaps had even gone looking for the girl)—decides to pay me a visit. He came in, smoking, in his robe with a snifter of brandy. We chatted and said it would be a nice night for us all to go out for a walk. A walk? Dad, it's 5 A.M.! I tried to get rid of him, saying, "What about Shirley?" His attitude was like, "Who wants to talk to Shirley? She needs her beauty sleep." I couldn't get rid of him. So the three of us talked in my room, awkwardly enough. When he finally left, around eight in the morning, the girl left with him. Instead of being discreet, my dad was pretty blatant about what he was up to. I really felt sorry for him. He appeared to be in such pain. He looked so wounded. The next day the girl told him she'd had sex with me—which probably sent him further over the edge.

I could see my dad was falling apart. When I got back to Los Angeles, I met with my manager to talk about him. Ruth was as concerned as I was—and in fact had been for quite some time. And she'd seen a lot more worrisome behavior on his part than I had. She said that sometimes he'd say things that simply didn't make sense, and he was losing his professionalism, which wasn't at all like him. There were nights when he would start winging it onstage, ad-libbing monologues, putting Shirley in an untenable position. We didn't know what to do. He was a ticking time bomb.

Things reached a head one weekend in Las Vegas. He'd been having terrible vocal problems, which weren't helped by his smoking several packs of cigarettes a day. He was drinking too much and had been losing money heavily, gambling. The pressures were too much. He went mad. One night after the show he locked Shirley in her room—perhaps so he could pursue his activities with the girl he liked without risk of interference. During the show, he appeared to suffer a complete breakdown, singing things that had nothing to do with anything. He was filming *The Eiger Sanction* during the day and the schedule was too much for him. He began taking pills to wake up and pills to sleep. He lost his voice and began missing shows. Shirley found him curled up in the corner of his room—nude—unable to carry on.

Ruth sent an associate, Howard Boris, our business manager, to Las Vegas to deal with the situation and bring my father back home. The hotel removed my father's name from the marquee. For the rest of the week it would simply be "The Shirley Jones Show," which wasn't easy for Shirley to deal with, since my father had created their whole show based around the two of them and their marriage.

What happened next, I didn't witness. Boris had hired a small plane and got my father into it. They were up in the air for twenty minutes without my father saying anything or acting in the least bit peculiar. He was dead calm. Then he unstrapped his seat belt, leaped over the seat, grabbed the controls from the pilot, and started screaming, "I'm going to see my father!" The pilot freaked!

Howard Boris went white, yelling, "Jack, Jack! You're going crazy! Stop it! You're going to kill us!" They wrested my father away from the controls and strapped him back in his seat. He went into a trance from there.

The next day my father was sighted watering the lawn in the middle of the afternoon—stark naked. Picture him, his tool hanging down to his knees, sharing himself with his presumably admiring public.

Ruth flew to the house. She found him standing atop a coffee table, pounding on a Bible, going, "J.C.—don't you get it? Jack Cassidy, Jesus Christ—they're both J.C. Don't you see? I'm me, J.C." He'd never been into the Bible before in his life. He had told my brother Shaun to read the Bible to him, which Shaun did, for as long as my father wanted. He had lit every fireplace in the house and refused clothes.

Ruth sent for the doctor, the one who had prescribed Valium, who she figured could handle any situation. She told him Jack had gone out of control. And the doctor hurried to the house to deal with my father. He was ready to sedate him. But my father—and this, I think, is the best, the most sane thing my father could have done—physically resisted. He called him a quack. When the doctor approached him, my father picked him up and threw him down so forcefully that the doctor dislocated a shoulder. The doctor had my father committed (against my father's will) to a mental hospital. The men in the white coats sedated my father, put him in a straitjacket, and carried him off. This was grist for the supermarket tabloids. *The National Tattler*, giving him the amount of attention he'd never before received in his career, screamed (December 22, 1974): "Jack Cassidy Cracks Up, Enters Mental Hospital. Wife Shirley Jones Forced to Commit Him."

They held him in the hospital for forty-eight hours, which is, I was told, as long as he could legally be held against his will for observation, since once he calmed down he was lucid, rational, and appeared to pose no harm to anyone.

A week or so afterward, acting as if nothing untoward had happened, he called me up and asked me to have lunch with him at Scandia. That turned out to be horrible—the most uncomfortable lunch I've ever endured. He'd been drinking. He was bloated. He started doing this song-and-dance charm routine I'd seen him do so many times, on so many people. But there was no way I was going to let him charm me anymore. His timing was way off. He tried to act like he was my father and we had this unbreakable father-son bond. But it was too late to be with someone to whom he'd never really been a parent. He couldn't use any of the usual parental power plays on me; he couldn't manipulate me into helping him, because I was more clever than he by then. I was now holding the upper hand. He had no credibility with me. There wasn't anything I needed from him. I didn't really want to be around him anymore.

He said, "Shirley and I have been having our problems." I suppose he expected me to feel sympathy for him. I knew he'd been sleeping with other women. He'd done it in front of me, even back when I was a teenager. He brought other women around and didn't even try to be discreet. I used to think, *Come on, Dad. This is poor showing.*

I knew something was coming. We hadn't seen each other since his nervous breakdown. But he didn't talk about that. He said he had gambling debts, adding, "I don't want to tell Shirley about this. I don't want to hurt her." He knew I loved Shirley and wouldn't want to hurt her by saying anything to her either. Finally he got to the point: "I need to borrow ten thousand dollars from you."

I looked at him and said, "Dad, I'd love to help you. You know what? I don't have any money." Which was a lie. But he was in such a state of craziness I knew that if I loaned him $10,000, he would just be using me, too. I knew that giving him the money would contribute to him spinning further out. I knew that it would be like burning $10,000, and I didn't want to open the door to this, because I knew it would be the first request of many. I wondered how many other people he was hitting up for money. That was the last time I saw him alive. He never called me again. I heard from Shaun that he was mad at me. I knew him so well.

Early in 1975 he and Shirley got divorced on grounds of "irreconcilable differences," although my father continued to insist to interviewers after the divorce that he still loved Shirley. Shirley began dating—and soon married—comedian Marty Ingels. I stopped seeing her at that time because I didn't get along with her new husband. I stopped seeing my father because I felt I'd taken just about enough abuse from him for one lifetime, although deep down I held a hope that he would change and one day we could have the relationship I used to long for.

It was painful for me, steering clear of him, because as a kid I'd really always wanted him to be my dad, to love me, and to want to be with me. And even though we grow up and we look like adults, we still have the same emotional needs. I still suffered from feeling rejected by my father as a kid. I still felt a sense that I was, in some fundamental way, not good enough and had deserved his neglect of me. So it was less painful for me simply to avoid him.

New York Post columnist Earl Wilson, interviewing my father November 12, 1975, as my father prepared to open in a new Broadway play, asked him if he saw much of me. "No. His crowd doesn't even know me. I don't talk about him because the interviews with me turn out to be about him. I have another son, Shaun, 16. He's a singer and a composer, and he has a hell of a chance to take off," my father said.

I had no contact with him at all in the last nine months of his life. He crossed me off his list, along with his sister and brother; they would call me and say, "What did we do? Why doesn't your father call us? What's wrong with him?"

I'd say, "He doesn't call me, either. Dad's crazy."

"Don't say that about your father!" they'd tell me.

The funny thing is, I thought I was just being clever, making up an excuse when I told my father I didn't have any money. But surprise, surprise. The world was about to make me swallow a big bad reality pill.

I had never worried about how much money I had. For years, I had just kept making more. My business managers always spoke glowingly of the wise investment moves they were making on my behalf. That was the one thing that counterbalanced all the hell I'd gone through in the last five years: at least I'd made a lot of money. I believed I was set for life, and could stay "retired" for as long as I chose. As far as I knew, I was simply worth millions, and—due to astute investments—my wealth was just there for me. I was so fucking trusting and naive.

But I never kept tabs on how much money was coming in and going out. The bills all went to my business manager. I didn't write checks. I didn't have the time. I figured that's what business managers were for. I had no business education whatsoever. Nobody in my family had any sophistication when it came to investments; they came from working-class backgrounds. So there wasn't anybody in my family tending the store, for any of us. We were all out, busily making money and putting it in the till. Until one day we looked—and discovered that the till had been raided.

I really can't blame Ruth. She came from a wealthy family. Ruth, like most women of her generation and socioeconomic class, simply had not been raised to worry about money. After the death of her brother, who'd headed the business end of Aarons Management, she'd hired business managers. Unwittingly, she went from one thief or incompetent to the next. That wound up costing my dad, Shirley, and myself a fortune.

One guy simply ran off with millions of our money. Another wasn't investing it where he thought it would do us the most good; he was investing it wherever he could get the biggest kickbacks—after first, apparently, skimming off the top. We also didn't have any money in tax shelters, which meant we had to needlessly pay a fortune to the IRS. I was in the 70 percent tax bracket in 1971. (In one year I paid the IRS more than $400,000; a good business manager could have legally avoided most of that tax obligation.) A light should have gone on in my head that I didn't have the best business management in the world the day one of the managers showed me I had a million dollars in a checking account. Maybe he wanted to impress upon me that my money was safe and sound, which it wasn't. I wasn't educated enough to realize that there was no reason I should have had that much money simply sitting in that checking account, not even earning interest!

For three years I invested heavily in oil, or so I thought. I was certain to make a fortune, right? Wrong. Do you remember the Home Stake Oil deal? That was one of the biggest scams in the history of the United States. Even some members of Congress were among the victims. It resulted in the largest class-action suit in history in America. An operation so fraudulent that at one point the perpetrators were actually painting water pipes orange to convince gullible investors the pipes were filled with oil. In the Home Stake Oil deal I was one of the top-ten biggest money-losers in the country. I got burned really bad, losing hundreds of thousands of dollars. My father and Shirley also got burned, but nothing like I did.

All told, millions of dollars of my money and my father's and Shirley's money were squandered and lost and invested poorly. It's a shame that my family and I never had the proper guidance. Even Ruth Aarons wound up getting suckered out of a lot of her money. We all got taken to the cleaners. It's a sad and too familiar story about Hollywood business managers and their wealthy celebrity clients.

What's the quote? The hardest thing in the world isn't to make a million dollars. It's to hold on to two dollars.

We sued the one business manager who admitted taking kickbacks. He could have gone to prison. But he was an old man and we settled out of court in exchange for his simply paying back to us money he'd taken in kickbacks. But we let him off way too easily.

The people who wronged me, taking advantage of a naive young guy—I can never forgive. I'll never again be in the situation I was when I was twenty to twenty-four years old. The chance of having an opportunity to earn that kind of money again—I don't care who you are—will almost never present itself again. That's just a fact.

Don't get me wrong; I wasn't cheated out of *all* my money. In 1975 I wasn't broke. But I realized I'd needlessly lost much of what I'd worked so hard to earn, which I'd never be able to recoup. And that harsh reality only further fueled my depression.

One of the few friends to whom I gave a lot of access in 1975 was Elliot Mintz. He proposed writing an authorized biography of me, saying it could make us both some money, as well as giving me a chance to get a lot off my chest. I spent many hours with him, letting him ask any questions he wanted, all of which I answered candidly to provide background for the book. I'd never before been interviewed in such depth; I told him that was the last interview I ever expected to do. I'm glad I taped my recollections of my career right then while they were all so recent, because those tapes helped me refresh my memory when the time came to do this book. Over the course of about a year, Mintz tried to find a publisher interested in a book on David Cassidy. But no one, in 1975 or '76, had any interest in me. I was considered old news, my music "dated." Disco was the new rage in pop music.

The arrival of disco in '76 also made my highly successful former record producer Wes Farrell passé. He didn't understand it; he couldn't change with the times. And this man, who had been mega-successful throughout the late sixties and early seventies—his stream of big hits with me and the Partridge Family had earned him an award as Producer of the Year—found suddenly nobody seemed to want him. When he had been making all the big bucks, and assumed that it would go on like that for years, he had spent lavishly. He bought the house on Sunset Boulevard and put two Rolls-Royces in the driveway: the California dream realized. He did everything by the book of how a man blows it. He wound up deeply in debt. He married Tina Sinatra, Frank's daughter, and I heard he managed somehow to get on Frank's bad side, which was in itself a big mistake. He left town. Broke.

Meanwhile, I was staying home, trying to keep the harsh realities of life outside at bay. But news from outside, too often not good, had a way of invading my sanctuary.

Late on the night of February 12, 1976, a male assailant plunged a knife into the chest of Sal Mineo near Mineo's apartment at 8563 Holloway Drive. Mineo was heard by a neighbor screaming, "Help! Help! Oh my God," before he died and his attacker fled. He was thirty-seven. Elliot Mintz handled the press, striving to ensure that Mineo's privacy was respected as much as possible after death. The police, knowing of Mineo's lifestyle, originally specu-lated that the crime had been sex-related, but when the assailant was finally apprehended more than a year later, it turned out that he was merely a common thief, who hadn't even known who Mineo was when he killed him with a five-dollar knife.

I blotted out reality by immersing myself deeper in drugs, alcohol, and music.

The night of Saturday, December 11, 1976, started out like any other for me. Some musician friends dropped over to party and jam with Steve and Sam and me. We stayed up most of the night, playing music. Because that was such an unhappy period of my life, I spent as much time as I could out of me—being in the zone, I used to call it. We were all pretty wiped out, emotionally and physically, by night's end. Numb. It was just a very dark, empty period of time for me. I always wanted to keep the party going, so I didn't have to go to sleep, so I didn't have to be alone, so I didn't have to deal with real life.

About five o'clock in the morning, after we'd stopped playing, I still felt too wired to call it a night. We had the radio on in the background. I was just bullshitting with Steve, sort of half listening to the news on the radio, when the newsman announced it had just come over the wire that actor Jack Cassidy had apparently died in a fire that had swept through his apartment. His body had been so badly charred, however, that it had not yet been possible to make a positive identification. Silence. Was I dreaming this? I looked at Steve. He looked at me and said, "Oh, shit."

I picked up the phone and I called my brother Shaun. No answer. I called my stepmother, Shirley. No answer. I called their service and I waited for a callback. I didn't believe it. It must have been nine or ten o'clock, a long time, before anyone called me back. I talked with Shaun. They had been out, trying to identify the body which had been so thoroughly burned that an absolute identification was only possible through dental records. I just listened. I wouldn't believe it . . . yet.

I drove over to the house. Part of me really didn't want to accept he had died until I opened the door, looked across the room, and saw all of my brothers—I realized suddenly that there was no one left except me and my brothers—at which point it felt as if someone thrust me down to the ground. I completely collapsed. I wailed my eyes out. I wept like a child, which I was.

My brothers and I all held each other in our arms. I remember saying things like, "It's just us now. His job here is over. This is what we were meant to do. We just have each other." I felt so much stronger because my brothers were there. And it's been like that with us ever since. We have a bond.

We didn't know much about his death at first. There seemed some uncertainties connected with it, and that bothered me. The police asked an awful lot of questions in an attempt to reconstruct his final night. He had dinner with actress Nanette Fabray and her husband. After he'd called it a night with them, he apparently went out to meet some guys for drinks. Although he'd told interviewers shortly before his death that he'd quit smoking and drinking, that did not seem to be the case. It appeared that he got drunk with them that night. Later, back in his apartment, he lit a cigarette but apparently fell asleep or passed out on the couch, which then caught fire. His body was found on the floor, as if he'd been trying to crawl to the apartment's sliding glass door when he passed out for good, death due to smoke inhalation.

But some believed there was more to his death than met the eye. Syndicated columnist Liz Smith, for example, reported (March 2, 1977), "The Los Angeles police have not closed the book on the tragic death by fire of that wonderful actor Jack Cassidy. . . . The dapper Jack loved to gamble and there are those who believe he was heavily in debt to the mob. To add to the mystery, two unsavory type guys were seen at his apartment earlier and a young woman who had been visiting the actor contends that he was safely tucked in bed when she left him. So why did Jack get up and move to the couch? And was his death an accident or wasn't it?" I believe it was.

What some of the columnists knew and the police investigators knew, but the public did not know, was that my father was bisexual.

The police concluded that on his last night my father went out drinking with some homosexual friends; they were unsuccessful in their research, however, to learn the identity of the person who had last seen my father alive.

Though I'd heard some rumors, I never really knew of my father's bisexuality—although apparently a lot of other people did—until after he died. Certainly he never discussed it with me, although he could have been open with me had he chosen to. But I guess, in some ways, he was very private. I can understand that.

My brothers and I have talked about it. Thinking back upon it, the idea that my dad may have been bisexual makes perfect sense. I mean, even though he never said anything about it, I can see it. It fits with the man I knew.

I'm not violating any privacy now in discussing my father's sexual interests, inasmuch as others have already made it public.

Cole Porter, for example, shared with his friend, writer Truman Capote, details of his extended sexual relationship with my father. In Gerald Clarke's best-seller, *Capote: A Biography*, Capote is quoted as saying how Porter described "his long affair with that actor Jack Cassidy."

Of course, my father revered Cole Porter and Cole knew it, which I'm sure made the keep-it-cool psychological power-playing stuff more palatable. Being close to Cole Porter, one of this country's most important writers of Broadway and Hollywood scores—especially when my father was a young, aspiring singer and actor—could only have helped my father's career. My father was definitely guilty of creating himself and of doing whatever it would take to get ahead. So he may have had some opportunistic motives there, in addition to sexual and affectional ones.

In Boze Hadleigh's book *The Vinyl Closet*, *Dance Magazine* editor William Como confessed that when Jack Cassidy—in his eyes, I guess, an unapproachable star—made a pass at him, he initially thought "it had to be a joke," but it soon led to a "scorching affair." Como said of my father (whom he found quite vain): "He loved the show-biz whirl, and he loved seducing VIPs of both sexes even if he had no intention of bedding them."

Well, Como had my father's number, all right. My father definitely did like to seduce people—but not just VIPs. I don't mean necessarily sexually; I don't know everyone my father may or may not have slept with. But if you saw him in action, it was as if he flirted with the whole world. Psychologically my father was seducing people all the time—whether they were elevator operators, doormen, or even room service guys. He would be at his most charming, his most beguiling, with all sorts of people, who were often surprised at the great attention he paid to them. Even though he was a big guy, it was important to him that these guys—like some fellow just bringing up the room service—all thought of him as grand, and felt like he personally considered them important. My father was great at making even a bellboy feel he was the most important guy in the world. Could that seductive behavior have sometimes led to sex, as people have suggested? Who knows?

I was sorry I didn't see my father for the last nine months of his life. I really regret not saying, "You know, Dad, I really love you, and I'm really sorry." But I was able to do that after he died.

As it turned out, my father had one final gesture of rejection to make toward me. The will was read. My father left me the big goose egg. I mean, I was cut out of his will, which placed his estate at $100,000. It made news that he had excluded both Shirley and me. Maybe my father decided we were rich and could take care of ourselves. Or maybe he wanted to pay us back for how he felt we'd treated him. But he left us nothing—not even any token gifts. He cut his brother and nephews in for 12.5 percent of his estate apiece. In the end, though, the lawyers and the taxes and everything ate up most of the estate. They had an auction of his clothes. I didn't go. I bought my father's pocket watch, before the auction, just to have something to remember him by. I paid $1,000 for it. Then it was stolen by someone close enough to me to have access to my home; I can't prove who did it, but I have some strong suspicions. I really would like to have kept that watch. My son would have had something of his grandfather's.

The desire to anesthetize myself was already pretty strong in me when my dad died—but his dying doubled my desire to make the pain go away. That was such a horrible time in my life. I just retreated further into myself.

My father's death was also a terrible blow to Ruth Aarons. They had been close for more than a quarter of a century. She began noticeably deteriorating, both psychologically and physically. I don't know that she had many friends, other than her small (and dwindling) pool of clients. Now my father was dead. And I was retired. I resisted her periodic overtures that I try to go back to work, which she felt would have been good for me—as well, of course, as good for her. I didn't mind visiting her when I could, to try to help buck her up (though I was bothered by the hundreds of pills she had at her home). But I rebuffed her suggestions that I go back to work, even when she tried to get me to do a proposed TV show called *The Hardy Boys*. Ruth received a further blow when Shirley decided to leave her. Who did she have left? Her world was shrinking.

She had one last hurrah as a personal manager. In 1977 she launched the career of my brother Shaun. She wasn't sure if they could get lightning to strike twice, but they did. His career trajectory followed much the same path mine did. Although it didn't last long, for a couple of years he had enormous success on TV, on records, and in concerts. From 1977 to '79 he starred in *The Hardy Boys*, the same show Ruth had spoken to me about doing. (It would have been a trip if we could have worked together; as it turned out, we had to wait 15 years before ever performing together, in the Broadway production *Blood Brothers*, which we are doing now.) He had three platinum albums in 1977 and '78, and five hit singles. He donned the tight white jumpsuits and shook his backside at screaming young girls, just as I had. His face appeared on posters, magazine covers, and lunch boxes. *Rolling Stone* even profiled him, before the fever ran its course. He retired from recording four years after he began.

For a while, when Shaun's career first began happening, it must have seemed like old times for Ruth—having another Cassidy become a teen idol. This time, she vowed, we won't make the mistakes we made the last time; we'll keep a careful eye on marketing and all the rest. She meant well, but the drugs had taken too great a toll on her. Shaun needed a manager he could feel confident in; he saw her failing, due to her drug addiction. He felt she was losing her mind, and he bailed out.

All of Ruth's clients left her in the end. I'd visit her a couple of afternoons a week. She wouldn't leave her bed. She didn't have the energy. She was so drugged from all the Seconals she took, she was just out of it. She'd tell me things like, "I *have* to take the pills; I have a terrible backache"—the rationalizations of an addict. Her muscles atrophied; it was such a shame, this vibrant person becoming so weak.

Then one day I got a call from Lloyd Brown, a man who worked for her. Apparently she had slipped in the shower, hit her head, and died. She took so many drugs, it was perhaps almost inevitable something tragic would happen. When she died, there were thousands of pills in her home.

CHAPTER
21

In 1977 I married Kay Lenz, a sweet, bright, beautiful actress whom I'd known for all of six weeks. What did we have in common? We'd both just recently lost our fathers, we were both feeling lost and lonely, and we were both actors—with all of the insecurities and self-absorption that seemed to go with the occupation. We were two lost souls. We made each other laugh. That sounded good enough to me.

By the time Kay and I met, she had already done more than twenty different TV shows, including the acclaimed miniseries *Rich Man, Poor Man.* She'd won an Emmy and had been nominated for another, not to mention a couple of other awards. When we married, I had not been working at all for a couple of years. So I'd stay home; she'd go off each day to work. It's funny how life works; I was now in much the same situation my father had been in, years before, being married to a highly in-demand actress who was the household's principal money-earner. This didn't last long for us, though.

Kay and I, unfortunately, had gotten married for the wrong reasons. We were both immature and we really weren't compatible as mates. It became apparent almost as soon as we'd gotten married that she wanted much less emotional involvement than I did. I felt I gave up a lot the day I married her. I gave up being old "Jack the Lad" with countless women and the freedom to do anything I wanted. And Kay, I discovered to my dismay, was actually kind of disinterested in me. Her career, I soon realized, definitely came first in her life. I thought, *What irony! I marry the one woman who doesn't want me.*

It seemed wrong, just staying home all the time while Kay went to work. I'd see Kay consider different scripts and think, *Gee, I used to do that. And I liked doing that.* So, a couple of months after we got married, I let it be known in the business that I was available as an actor again. And there were old friends who remembered me. Former *Partridge Family* producer/director Mel Swope was, by this point, producing a dramatic anthology series, *Police Story*, and he offered me a role guest-starring in "A Chance to Live," an episode that aired May 28, 1979, on NBC. It was a two-hour movie. I did some press to promote my work. The headline above James Brown's piece in the *New York Post* was typical. It read, "Cassidy: Time Ripe for Comeback." Another line promised "A Look at a Teen Heart-throb's Return." I explained to Brown how, by the end of doing *The Partridge Family*, "I was emotionally and physically drained. I was all used up," and for several years thereafter, "I wasn't sure I ever wanted to work again. But there's something to be said about getting up in the morning and having something to do."

I received an Emmy nomination as Best Dramatic Actor for my performance. That was enough to convince NBC and Screen Gems that I might be worth gambling on for another series. They persuaded me the following week. Could my old popularity be revived?

I managed to pick up a few other odd movies for television over the next few years (all, incidentally, on my old *Partridge Family* network, ABC). But Kay got far more work than I did. In the 1970s and '80s she made sixty-odd TV appearances, guest-starring in one top series after another and also starring in such made-for-TV movies as *The Initiation of Sarah, Escape, The Hustler of Muscle Beach, The Seeding of Sarah Burns*, and *Sanctuary of Fear*. So—thanks in no small part to Kay—we continued to make a pretty good living. With her money and mine, we began speculating in Southern California real estate. The problem was, we got in when the market was just about reaching its peak. When the bottom fell out, around 1980, we lost a fortune. How much? Our mortgage payments alone were over $15,000 a month. It would take me all of the 1980s to pay off bank loans. I would have to say that the boom and crash in the real estate market wiped us out of almost everything.

Besides speculating in real estate, for many years I also indulged my passion for breeding thoroughbred racehorses. Though I still love horses, I'm essentially out of the racehorse game now because I know I cannot stand the pain and frustration any longer. It seemed like I had a number of chances to really hit the jackpot with horse racing but somehow I never did. It always eluded me. The best horses I owned would break their legs or something else with a one-in-a-thousand chance of happening would happen. Breeding and racing horses turned out to be a lot of heartache and disappointment.

As, ultimately, did my marriage to Kay. Looking back, I think we should have just stayed friends and never married. From the very beginning, ours was not really a successful marriage. And the strains of our mounting financial worries certainly didn't help matters.

I must also note that Kay was not prepared for my old fans,

some of whom kept coming on to me—sometimes right in front of Kay. (Incidentally, that situation still occurs, with women hitting on me right in front of my current wife, Sue Shifrin. It gets embarrassing.) So there were a lot of stresses on our marriage; I knew early on that my marriage was in trouble. It was good for my head to connect once in a while with an old friend.

Between 1970 and '74, I had made about $8 million—virtually all of which was gone by 1980. I know, $8 million might not sound like a lot of money now, but don't forget—in the early seventies a house on Beverly Drive that today would cost $6 million was selling for $125,000. By 1980 my net worth was less than $100,000. That to me was dead broke.

More than that, my career was in the toilet. I had trouble getting anyone at my agency, which had been handling me since the early 1970s, to even return my phone calls. If you're not a big moneymaker anymore, it's as if they don't want to know you, and no one in Hollywood seemed eager to hire David Cassidy any longer.

Okay, I had retired from the business. But now I was back and I really needed work. Yet nobody at William Morris seemed to feel they had any kind of moral obligation or loyalty to me. No one said that because I'd been such a huge money-earner for them in the 1970s, they'd make sure I'd get work now that I needed it. They simply didn't give a flying fuck about me or my career.

I went in to see the head of the agency, Sam Weisbord. He bullshitted me about what a champion I was, and how I had the blood of champions; he had great respect for my whole family. He pointed over to their new wing, saying, "It's because of you and your family that we were able to build that wing."

I thought, *That's great. That's really wonderful. Our family made a lot of money for you. Now what are you going to do to help me?*

I needed work not just for financial reasons, but for my mental well-being. In 1981 Kay and I separated, leading to the divorce we knew was inevitable the following year. If my personal life was not gratifying, it was essential to me that my professional one be.

My agency got me one final decent job before our relationship came to an end. They figured Broadway would be the place for me to make a comeback.

In 1981 I went out on the road for a pre-Broadway tour of a new production of George M. Cohan's *Little Johnny Jones*. Believe me, that was one tough role—singing and dancing to classic Cohan songs that we've all seen James Cagney do superbly when he portrayed Cohan on-screen in *Yankee Doodle Dandy*. However, critics didn't think I was ready to step into Cagney's—or Cohan's—shoes. Let's face it, no one was. Before the show made it to Broadway, where it quickly died, the producers replaced me with Donny Osmond. In the months of our pre-Broadway tour, we did boffo business, I was paid well, but by year's end I had nothing to show for it. God, what I wouldn't have done, over the years, for some good financial advisors.

I picked up what work I could in regional theater, including a production of *Tribute*, written by *Partridge Family* creator Bernard Slade—a loyal friend from the old days.

In 1983 I finally did get back to Broadway, but I can't say I made any great waves. I replaced Andy Gibb in the leading role of Andrew Lloyd Webber and Tim Rice's hit show *Joseph and the Amazing Technicolor Dreamcoat*, which had opened the year before. The show was going to close until I joined it, but once again my fans came in droves, and I stayed the entire six-month run.

In 1984 I moved to England and started writing new songs and recording for MLM/Arista Records. My single "Last Kiss" rose to number 6 on the British charts in March of 1985. "Romance (Let Your Heart Go)" made it to number 54 in May. That same month, my album *Romance* reached number 20 on the British album charts, and I had a sold-out British concert tour. None of my recordings, however, made any impact whatsoever in the United States. They were never released in the U.S. by Arista in America.

I was frustrated in that no matter what I tried, a real successful comeback never seemed to materialize for me. Sometimes I'd feel I was truly close. It was clear as I toured that I had a loyal audience. I'd made a hit record but I just didn't have the needed support and follow-through from others. I had no management to speak of anymore. I went through several managers, none of whom were committed to me the way the late Ruth Aarons had been, or worked toward long-term career building. They just wanted to make some quick money off me, which of course they did.

My record companies kept seeming to disintegrate under me. In 1985, the very week that my new album *Romance* on Arista Records made the Top 20 in England, BMG acquired Arista and fired the whole staff at Arista. So there was nobody there to promote the album. I dropped off the charts immediately. Something like that happened to me again in 1990. It looked like I had a real hit in the making with an album and single released on the Enigma label, here in America—I actually broke into the Top 40 in America, for the first time in eighteen years—but the company just fell apart. And without a strong company behind you, pushing your record, stores aren't going to stock it and disc jockeys aren't going to play it. My relationships with record companies have always been, at best, frustrating.

In the mid-eighties I got married again. There's not much to say about my second marriage, to a woman named Meryl Tanz, except that it didn't last too long—from 1984 to 1986. We didn't have much in common except that we both loved horses.

As I look back over my life, I'd say I began really spinning out, spiraling down, from about mid-1974, and stayed on a downward course for about a decade. Even though there were some bright moments in the late seventies and early eighties most of those years were spent in darkness. I don't know how to describe it, other than to say I felt a real darkness inside of me.

For all of those years—although it's painful to acknowledge—I was ashamed of who I was, where I'd come from, what I was about, and the mistakes I'd made. That I'd failed at marriage was, to my way of thinking, just another in a long line of failures.

I'm a failure. That was my core belief. Like being a failure had always been my real destiny in life or something. I'd get drunk and dwell on how far I'd fallen. The same thoughts would run through my mind, over and over. All of the things that hadn't worked out. And as I grew older and heavier, looking less and less like the youth whose face had once adorned T-shirts, posters, and cereal boxes, the chances of getting another chance seemed to grow more remote.

Emotionally I bottomed out in 1986. The record company had been taken over by BMG; the people I'd known were gone. I was getting divorced for the second time, just four years after the first marriage had failed. So I had two failed marriages and a failed career. Not bad, eh? I had a sense of not being able to enjoy anything that was working, not being able to gather any momentum. I'd go and do this and that. I'd work really hard and nothing would happen. I didn't see how I could carry on much longer.

I didn't want to be a star anymore. I just wanted to work—and I wasn't having much luck even doing that. I kept writing songs and sang them only to myself. I looked in vain for decent acting roles.

I wrote an album; it took me two years to write all of the songs on it. The album sank without a trace. I thought, *Gee, that was two years of my life, gone again.*

I felt lost, really and truly. Every day, I woke up with this darkness still inside of me. I kept thinking, *I'm not enough. I'm not talented enough. I'm not good enough. I'm not clever enough. I'm not young enough. I'm not tall enough. Every day, the world reminds me I'm not something else that I should be. I'm certainly not—though it's painful to admit—I'm not husband enough. I'm not man enough. I haven't been able to do that. I must not be good enough. I have never had a good enough relationship* . . . and on and on and on. I wallowed in thinking about all the ways in which I'd turned out to be a failure.

I knew I was smoking and drinking way too much. I even began to black out on a number of occasions. A classic sign of alcoholism. So I've learned.

My life was such a mess and I was personally in so much pain about everything else I had fucked up, from my career to my family. I beat myself up over the fact that I hadn't talked to my own father for the last nine months of his life, and now—even though I'd moved from London back to Los Angeles—I was no longer communicating with Shirley. I just couldn't stand Marty Ingels, the man she'd chosen to marry after my father. But I didn't have much of an emotional support system left.

I should make it clear, I wasn't estranged from my brothers. But my brothers were very involved in their own lives. Although they were sympathetic to what was going on in mine, they could offer nothing more than an occasional "Let's go play tennis" or "Let's go have lunch." "C'mon, Donk, you've gotta get rid of this anger and out of this funk."

When I suffered severe financial problems, no one in my family was in any position to help me out. None of my brothers had made that kind of money. They were all struggling to take care of themselves. By the mid-eighties my brother Shaun had a wife and three kids to support. His career was not exactly going very well at the time I was hitting bottom; he had his own problems to deal with. My brother Patrick was an actor trying to make a living himself. So there was really no money around. I had no one to turn to for help.

Shaun didn't make as much money from his handful of hit records as some might imagine. That's pretty much a myth about recording artists making a fortune from records. Most of the time the record companies make the money, not the artists. At least that's what every artist I've ever known has told me.

So by the mid-1980s I was broke and almost everything in my life was negative. I was depressed and withdrawn. Exactly how broke was I? When I left my second wife in 1986, I had accumulated nearly a half million dollars in debt. I left that marriage with less than a thousand dollars in my bank account. My only possessions were what I could carry out of the house. I didn't have a car. I didn't have a job. And no place to live. Yeah, I did a gooood job of wrecking my life, didn't I?

For a while, I lived with my ex-roommate, Sam Hyman, at his place. He and I had been so close for so many years, he welcomed me back into his life. He took me in again, even though I was a real mess at this time. I had no income. And I wasn't exactly fun company, folks. Hell, I could hardly stand being around myself. This is what is called hitting rock-bottom.

Then, for about six months, I lived in the guest bedroom of Sam's sister's two-bedroom apartment. She was rarely there, preferring to stay with a boyfriend. So there I was, once a highly paid superstar, living in a little place where I was paying $450 a month in rent. Stripped of everything I had owned, except the debt. I had no career. I had no prospects for a job. Filled with self-loathing and regret, I had just about completed the job of self-destruct. Nice work, Davey-boy!

My career certainly was not working in 1986. My debts only kept growing larger. My attorneys kept sending me bills. At the time, I got hit with a paternity suit, which made the *New York Post*'s notorious "Page Six." While the *Post* was printing the news of the paternity suit being filed against me, halfway around the world a sleazy little newspaper in Germany was printing an "exclusive interview" I'd supposedly given them, coming out as a homosexual. Incredibly, the story got picked up by a paper in England, then another. You try to deny something like that, you only wind up calling more attention to it. Most recently, it's even found its way into a book, which reported that I had revealed my homosexuality while in Germany. Hell, I hadn't even been in Germany at the time of the supposed interview. I was in L.A., struggling like hell to come up with another rabbit to pull from my hat.

But I couldn't worry much about what newspapers were or were not writing about me. That was the least of my concerns. In 1986, in almost every way imaginable, my life was just not working.

I was suicidal. I thought about it but I never had the courage. I think I also knew that I had the power to make it again. Everyone whose life is in pain has thought about it, I'm sure. But I never went through with it. Too much pride. I always saw suicide as the ultimate failure.

But I had fallen about as low as a person could fall. I had no possessions anymore. People still knew my name; they knew I had been a teen heartthrob many years before. But all that was ancient history. Nobody really cared about me anymore, professionally.

Meanwhile, I received an invitation to Aspen, Colorado, for a couple of days. Get out of L.A. and ski. Sounded too good to be true. While I was there, I ran into an old friend who said Don Johnson was in town, and was throwing a party with Bruce Willis. This friend said, "David, Bruce knows you're in town and wants you to come to the party. Your name will be in the list; you have to be 'fabulous' to get in. All Hollywood is going to be at this party."

Ah, yes, so I arrived at the party. There were only a dozen or so people there; I was one of the first to arrive. Don's holding court in a ridiculous mohair suit—it must have cost two grand! I walked up to Don. This was a guy who knew me from the beginning, who'd been to my home, an old, old friend. I feel close to people I go way back with. The last time I'd seen him, he'd driven up to my house in his beat-up old Volkswagen. I was thinking, *This is going to be great; I can tell him how happy I am for all his success.*

I said, "Don, how are you, man—great to see you," thinking how glad this old friend would be to see me.

He looked at me, smiled tightly for just a beat, and then went back to his conversation with somebody else. He absolutely iced me. I laughed, to try to break the tension, and said, "Don, you're kidding. Right?" Oh, my God, what an asshole.

He said, "Yeah," and laughed at me in a way—it was as if he were saying, "Yeah, aren't I an asshole?" And turned his back to me.

I went, "Don't fucking do this, Don." No response. "I don't fucking believe it," I said, and walked away, wondering, *Are you a human being anymore, Don? Are you real?* Was this what being a star meant for him? That now he could snub people he'd felt he'd risen above? Maybe in his mind that was his way of paying me back for getting jobs he wanted when we were both starting out. Maybe he didn't want this reminder of his early years hanging around. I don't know what goes through people's brains. I've witnessed how fame corrupts people. Well, at this time he was gone.

I was feeling a lot of pain because of my divorce, and so many other things. I just felt like I'd failed at everything. I'd done a lot in England, but nothing in America, where it really counted, my home. I'd felt lost many times in my life, but this time more than ever. I felt hypersensitive, kind of like an outsider coming back, trying to start my life and career over again. And to have Don snub me—I felt as if he were saying, *Hey, I never really rated you anyway,* or *I don't need you losers any longer.* At the time it hurt.

It seemed like a thousand people walked through the door, a

veritable who's who of showbiz. I walked out quietly. Alone. Nobody noticed I'd left, I'm sure . . . or if I'd been there at all.

Maybe most people in the business no longer cared about me. One did, however, and in 1986 I found someone to represent me as an agent who eventually became my manager, Melanie Green— and she still does care, theatrically. At that time, I was still drinking heavily. In fact, I was quite drunk the night I first met Melanie at a party in Los Angeles. She said she was a real fan of mine and had seen me perform in concert, and thought I was a good actor. I told her I was drunk and I told her I was also fundamentally a mess— facts that I'm sure she didn't need me to tell her. But she offered to represent me. And that, I think, marked the beginning of my professional recovery.

CHAPTER 22

What I have been able to do from 1987 until now—I'm talking about rebuilding my life, from the bottom up—I surely could not have done without my current wife, Sue Shifrin—the woman I stood up the Queen of England for, back in 1973. Little did I dream when I first met her that thirteen years later, after we'd both had unsuccessful marriages, we'd end up together.

What happened was, when I was at this complete low point in my life, I got a call from my attorney. Sue had contacted him and wanted to get in touch with me; she didn't know how else to reach me. I called Sue back, took her out to dinner, and since that night, we've been together ever since. Connecting with Sue really began to shift my life from the dark side back into the light. Just being around her—she was so positive, so supportive, so caring, so loving. Her whole attitude was so *I don't care that you're drunk, David; I don't care that you're a mess. And have no money.* When someone embraces you at your lowest point, it really means something. It carried a lot of weight with me.

And I could not have begun the rebuilding of my career without Melanie Green. I told Melanie that in 1984 and '85, I'd pretty much lived in England and had had a lot of success over there. I said I really wanted to do some acting again. And she got me an offer to replace Cliff Richard in the leading role (playing a rock star) of the London West End production of the musical *Time.* Because I was totally broke, I really needed that job. Yet even though I had less than a thousand dollars to my name, I turned down the first three offers the producer of *Time* made to me. I really played this poker hand well. As if I was still rich. And that's the only way that I've ever negotiated—from a sense of strength and power. I've always been willing to walk away from a deal if I didn't get what I felt I deserved. I began to take my power back, and I had someone to support me doing it and someone who loved me.

They paid me a lot of money to do the play. I must say that even though it was a hit, I thought *Time* was a bad play—no story really, no substance. It was just a poorly written star vehicle for anybody who could sing and had a little charisma. But it had incredible sets, lights, and special effects. And it was promoted extremely well. So, even though the play was really a piece of fluff, I had a great success with it. My fans came in droves. Business was terrific. And it helped give me my first step of a real comeback. As an adult.

With Sue's support, I made the decision to go into analysis at that time when emotionally, professionally, and personally I had pretty much bottomed out. I found my analyst through Sue, who had benefited greatly from analysis herself. Even though analysis is painful, it's not anywhere near as painful as living in the kind of misery I was experiencing. I just couldn't stand it any longer. I knew I must find a way to change to be happy with myself again.

I realized I needed to fix myself. What were my choices? I could either walk around and get drunk and be angry and bitter, or I could say, "As long as I'm here, I want to feel good."

So I began to concentrate on healing myself. I had to feel whole as a person, independent of whether there was a professional career for David Cassidy or not. My hope was that, through analysis, I could sort of rebuild my life; I didn't hold out any hopes for my career, which seemed to all intents and purposes dead. I really didn't begin changing as a person until the late 1980s, when I began analysis seriously. What a difference it made for me. Three and a half years, three times a week. Every week a little more light.

Thanks to the analysis, I stopped drinking during the run of *Time*. I stopped smoking cigarettes shortly afterward—and then, briefly, took up smoking big Cuban cigars. Which looked completely ridiculous, of course, but I absolutely loved them. Finally I quite smoking cigars, too. That was my last vice. I realized, smoking just didn't work for me. None of the old vices really did. I woke up one day and realized how much I loved myself and my life. How blessed I was.

I can't smoke, I can't drink anymore. (And I *don't* drink, except for perhaps an occasional light beer or half a glass of wine. It simply doesn't work for me.) I certainly can't do drugs. I hate the thought of them. I guess the only things left for me are cookies and milk. Well, okay, sex and cookies and milk. Not bad. But I feel better now than I did before I gave up those old vices. I mean, I look at what I am, which is pretty clean, pretty light—and pretty lucky.

I've been a chronic insomniac for as long as I can remember being alive. It comes and goes, is more or less intense depending on what's going on in my life. I'll lie awake in bed at night and think about choices I have to make. But if that's the worst of my problems these days, all right. I can live with that. But I'm still working on it. I'm doing meditation at night now. God, where is Steve?

I eat healthy foods. I'm not quite a pure vegetarian anymore. I mean, I now eat fish and fowl. I feel good. Hear that, Ma? Good!

I must say, I really believe I owe it to myself to wake up every morning and feel good. And whatever it's going to take for me to get there without interfering with anybody else's day—that's what I'm going to do. I'm gonna work at it, baby.

It feels good that I'm in a position again where I can do somebody else some good once in a while, too. My old buddy from *Partridge Family* days, Danny Bonaduce, got in some trouble with the law in 1990 for buying cocaine in Daytona Beach, Florida, and again in 1991 for beating and robbing a transvestite prostitute in Phoenix, Arizona, which really messed up the career he was trying to make for himself as a disc jockey. I've tried to stand by him. I believe in him. We've had many similar problems. But I've always believed in him as a man and in his talent.

I'm still like Danny's big brother. I've tried to help him to get his life together. He'd been almost out of control at the time of the arrests. His self-esteem was very low, which is why he's had so many problems. He has been very self-destructive. I really do like him and feel for him. I think he's a good person underneath that. He deserves forgiveness and support.

I think he sees me as something of a pain in the ass, this voice of good, you know. When I call him, he probably thinks, *Oh, fuck, here comes the medicine again*. But I'm one of the only people who gives a damn and will say anything to him about it. When he got arrested for the drug deal, I was the only person who called and asked, "What can I do to help? If you need something, I just want you to know I'm here, and I understand you've got a problem." When he was in jail, I was the one who called him.

He was blown away. Because he never felt worthy enough for anybody to care. I think he's still amazed that I will take the time to call him. I call him every few months just to find out how he's doing. Because there aren't that many people that give a shit about you in the world. But it's important. And he's worth saving. He's got a lot to give. I think he's genuinely gifted and very funny.

I really don't mean to be patting myself on the back here. Whatever I've done for Danny, I'm sort of doing for myself, too. And I simply do like talking with him. He's about the only one left that I can really reminisce with about the old days. Susan and I don't really talk anymore. The other kids in the cast were too young at the time to really know what was going on. Danny and I are friends, like peers.

He's working things out. He's gotten free of drugs and alcohol, and even helps raise money for rehabilitation programs. I've taken him out a couple of times, to open for me on my concert appearances. He's a terrific opening act for me. He's hysterical. So that's another what you might call selfish reason that I have for wanting Danny to stay well and thrive. He's the link to the past that was fun. But whatever comes in our lives, comes, you know. I can live with it.

So where am I today? I'm not a rich man. Yet I'm not complaining. I'm probably happier now than I've ever been before in my life.

I've learned a lot about life and about myself and how to distance myself from the parasites of this world. I know that there's sickness and illness and bad people out there and I'm not unscathed. I have been hurt, I have been disappointed, and I just chose no longer to indulge that. Even as I was working on this book, I learned that Elliot Mintz, whom I once considered one of my best friends, was trying to peddle to publishers—without my approval—the raw, unedited tapes of interviews I'd given him years ago as background for the book about me he once wanted to write.

My own take on life has gotten much more satisfying in recent years. I can simply cope with much more. Failures don't bother me the way they once did.

You see, I used to have an attitude about life that we were all in a race together and those of us who achieved the most success and the most fame and the most money and the most power were the winners. That isn't how I view life anymore. That view is for fools.

There is no race. There are no trophies. The only people who really win are the people who, when they awaken in the mornings, open their arms and get hugged by their loved ones; the people who can lie in bed at night, knowing they've really done right by themselves and whomever they love. The quality of my life is great because of the people that I have cultivated and that I choose to spend time with. I no longer have any time—not another minute, not another second—to waste with people who don't have that, don't share that, don't embrace that. So people who are false—I don't really have time to say anything more than: "No, I'm not interested. Thanks a lot but I really have to go. Sorry."

To go any further and to indulge them in their twisted view of reality—I can't expend any of my energy doing that. I had enough of that with my father and my bad relationships.

After five hard, long years of analysis, it felt like we finally hit the home stretch—I experienced some real breakthroughs. I realized that I had to let the reins go and let my life take me down whatever path was intended. The way I'd always kept trying to make the world go the way I wanted it to had not been working. The world was *not* going to go the way I wanted it to, and getting pissed off about it didn't help. I realized that if I would just accept the world and accept the way my life was intended to go, I would really see the riches, and see how lucky I really am.

Formerly I was caught up on a treadmill saying, "I've got to go here, I've go to get this part in the show, then I have to do . . ."

But today it's more like, "No. If I don't get a part I want, well, there's a reason for it." I have no great disappointments in my life anymore. Just enjoyment of the ride.

I used to go through a lot of: "Damn it, why didn't what I want happen?" "Why wasn't I able to get that film?" "Why didn't that series work?" "Why didn't I get this play?" "How come this record wasn't a hit?" And on and on. Who knows? Who cares?

I don't do that anymore. What I do now is really put myself in a mode of *What is the lesson for me in this one?* Instead of griping and grumbling, I'll tell myself, *Okay, I've worked for three months on this project, put everything I could into it, and it didn't happen.* Well, it was not intended to happen. Also, there were signs I should have seen early in the game. Now I realize that the attitude of *No, I'm going to make this work no matter what* doesn't work. That nothing *has* to happen. That I don't *have* to get any particular job if I'm to be happy or fulfilled. And if something fails to work out, it failed for a reason. There is something to be learned from the experience. Maybe it's worked out in a way that will ultimately be for my higher good. Maybe something better is meant to happen.

Perhaps I just missed getting on that plane because I was supposed to meet some stranger in the airport waiting room instead. Who knows? But I really view life like that now. I have developed a wisdom, and a sense of detachment to having it go the way I think I want it to go. Well, of course I still want things a certain way but it doesn't really *have* to go that way. There's a film I want to do. If I don't get to do it, I'll be slightly disappointed, but in a way I'll also feel lucky because—this is what I believe—something better will undoubtedly happen instead. Something else is meant for me. I'm happy with that.

I've given up trying to steer the ship and make it go the way I think it has to go. My attitude now is more like, *Okay, let's just see where this is going to take us.* Which allows me to enjoy the ride so much more. Now I just stand back and view it and say, *Look at how interesting this all is. Wow, you made all that money and you lost it all . . . So, let's see what's going to happen now.* For me, that's a better way to live. And it's worked.

I must admit, I don't have too many close friends in my life. But to tell you the truth, that's okay too. I spend a lot of time by myself. Time for myself is rare and precious, because I have a son and a wife, in addition to a very public career.

How do I fill my time these days, when not busy acting? I enjoy going to the theater, to movies, and to sporting events—probably the Rangers and the races or the Yankees would be my first choices. Occasionally I'll listen to sound track albums; occasionally I'll listen to some Gershwin. The sound track from *Manhattan*, for example, will put me in a good mood. And I'll read everything I can find pertaining to horses. I may not be involved in breeding and racing horses anymore, but at least I can read about them. I'm very brain-heavy concerning investments now, let me tell you.

I spend a lot of my time writing songs on the guitar. I wrote and recorded the theme song for *The John Larroquette Show* on NBC—it's a bluesy little song; whenever I pick up the guitar and just begin playing, it's always the blues. That's where my heart is, not in the kind of cheery pop music most people still associate with me. Incidentally, although *The John Larroquette Show* is written and produced by a friend of mine, I didn't get that gig out of friendship. I wanted my work to speak for itself, so I submitted the demo tape that I'd recorded under a pseudonym, Blind Lemon Jackson. The people who made the decision listened to the tape without knowing they were actually listening to David Cassidy.

Of course I try to spend as much time as I possibly can with my son, Beau, who is now almost three. I try to do everything with him that my father failed to do with me.

So, for example, before I left for the theater today (I'm in *Blood Brothers* on Broadway), I spent forty-five minutes with my son. And in those forty-five minutes we played the piano, I read him a story and worked on a puzzle with him. It really was quality time. So even forty-five minutes twice a day—and I'll see him longer than that if I can—is all it takes. He knows that I'm there for him and that's the most important thing. Even if I work a ten-hour day.

As an actor and singer, sometimes I have to protect my voice. I have to remain silent for major portions of the day, so I don't overtax my vocal cords. My son understands that I have to be silent. He knows it's nothing personal when I can't speak. Sometimes I'll whisper to him, rather than speak aloud. He'll whisper right back to me. We have our whispering sessions. Sign language with him is a ball.

And right now, appearing with my brother Shaun in *Blood Brothers* on Broadway is giving me about nine of the ten jolts you can possibly get from a creative project. It's been a terrific opportunity for both of us. We play twin brothers who've been raised apart; my character has grown up in a poorer home than Shaun's character, experiencing far more problems with his marriage, he loses his job, and his life falls apart. As you can imagine, I can relate.

My brother Patrick is also doing his part to keep the Cassidy acting tradition alive; he's appeared on the Broadway stage in *The Pirates of Penzance* and on-screen in *Longtime Companion*. I get along well with Shirley these days, and even Marty and I have formed a friendship. I'm very close with my family now, all of them. I have come a long way and still have a long way to go.

In 1993, "Nick at Nite" asked me to help them promote the Partridge Family show which they were planning to air in the summer. I told them I wanted very much to help them because I have come full circle with it. It's no longer an obstacle for me. It's an asset. It is a classic sitcom and for me it represents all the good times, not the artistic frustration. I finally got over the hump. I wanted people to hear me and see that I was okay with it. That I, too, loved it for what it was. I do. I've embraced it.

CHAPTER 23

The other day, I was asked if I'd be willing to speak to students at the high school in my old hometown, West Orange, New Jersey. I wasn't sure what I'd have to say, but I agreed to go out there. Aside from my mother, my cousin Barbara (who grew up and still lives in New Jersey), and my collaborator on this book, the audience was all kids. Kids, I'm sure, not all that different than I was when I lived in West Orange.

I spoke off the cuff, from the heart. "The last couple of days, what I've been going through—thinking about this, driving to this town again, seeing all of you . . . I have a connection to this town, but it's been thirty-five years. I'm going to try to find a place emotionally in me, where I can share some things with you," I began. I tried to caution them about drugs. Who doesn't? Thinking of my friend Kevin Hunter, who had died when we were teens, and how lucky I was not to have overdosed on drugs, considering all the drugs I used in my crazed days, and of River Phoenix, who'd recently succumbed to the same temptations I'd faced, I tried to tell them that if you become involved with drugs, you'll someday either quit or you'll die. But you're gonna pay.

I wanted to say something about how too many pressures can be put on young guys who haven't figured out what the world is yet. Something important about the lessons I've learned since I first got on board that Partridge Family bus. I don't think the kids wanted to hear that. We threw it open to questions and they wanted to know things like how I had become so successful—meaning how could they get some of the wealth and fame and popularity and (they were sure) happiness I'd gotten so fast. Kids are always going to have stars in their eyes.

The kids presented me with a West Orange High School football jersey, with my name on it. A couple of girls showed me their lockers; they had covered the insides with photos and clippings about me. That blew me away. I had heard about girls doing that to their lockers, back in the old days, but I'd never actually seen one until now. A couple of the boys asked if they could get a picture with me. "And would you like me to sign an autograph for you?" I asked. "Well, actually," one of the boys asked, "what would make a really cool picture would be if you were asking us for *our* autographs." Which I think puts hero worship in its proper perspective. We took the pictures.

Afterward, my collaborator and I got in his big old Lincoln and drove around the town. Past Tory Corners, where my grandfather bought me a Slinky and a Mr. Machine, so many years ago. Past the homes of childhood friends. Past the Catholic school that all the kids on my block except me went to. Past what used to be the public school that I went to (it's now used for board of ed offices). We stopped at my old house, which hasn't changed much;

they were still even using the clothesline in the back. I remembered those kids who'd taunted me as I'd played out front.

And we headed back to New York, where I'm currently living. There are quicker ways to drive to New York from West Orange now than there were when I was a kid. But my collaborator, a Jersey boy himself, didn't take Route 280 or any of the other newer roads. Without saying anything, he went the old way. We talked of Kevin Hunter and Ruth Aarons, and others from my past, as we drove.

Then I realized where we were. "This is Route 3, isn't it?" I asked. He nodded. We were very near the spot where my father, in that shiny new Cadillac that was just *so Jack*, had casually shattered my world with the news that he and Mom were divorced, and had been divorced for a couple of years. I remembered. I remembered the exact spot.

And I realized that I'd made my peace with old Jack Cassidy— I hadn't exactly forgiven him, but I'd made my peace with him. There were no ghosts I needed to do battle with here.

A car pulled up close alongside of ours. The driver honked and signaled for me to lower my window, while he lowered his.

"We saw you in *Blood Brothers*," said the guy, who looked to be about my age. The woman sitting alongside of him added cheerfully, "We love your work." And they drove off.

I liked that. It's kind of nice now, being recognized. I used to hate it when I was young, but it's good now. I guess I've made peace with a lot of things.

Can I confess something? I even enjoy—I honestly do—singing all the old songs that in 1974 I was sure I'd never want to sing again. I can't explain it. For some of those Partridge Family–era songs were ones that I'd never have recorded back then, had I been given any choice. They're songs I'd never choose to record now. And yet I realize that they brought their share of happiness to people. And I liked that. I liked it when people of my generation tell me I've had some kind of a positive impact on their lives. It means a lot to me.

So I'll sing the old songs that I felt weren't "me" when I first recorded them, because they're a part of my history now, and of a lot of other people's history, too. And I'll sneak in a few of the funky blues that for some reason really felt like "me" when I was fourteen, fifteen, sixteen—and still do today. I'm gonna do a tune next summer and send myself and the 1970s up. "Summer of Camp."

Who cares if I'm all grown up? I guess I'm supposed to impart here some of the very adult wisdom that I've acquired along the way. But you want to know something? I still feel like a teenager inside. Maybe more so now than when I was playing a teenager, during those *Partridge Family* years, when people had me working eighteen hours a day, seven days a week. I have time to play a little now, as I did when I was a teen.

I don't know how much I've changed. People tell me, "You have no agenda with your past or with your fame, do you?" And I don't, really. It put me through hell, yes, but I'm doing all right now. I really am. I made it, Daddy!

I don't wear a suit and tie or look like I'm an executive at a bank. We all have crosses to bear. If mine is that I'm going to be this eternal kid, I can live with that. There's a part of me that feels very much that way. I like it that people still want me to perform. I kind of like it that I can still strap on the guitar and still have fun. Acting is fun. I enjoy it more now than I did then. And I appreciate that people still care about my work.

"So . . ." somebody asked me the other day with a hint of disapproval in his voice, "when are you going to give up this 'David Cassidy teenager' thing?" Huh?

"I don't know," I told him, surprised by the question. And I grinned. "I'm having too much fun to give it up now."